W9-DJN-983

Δ The Triangle Papers: 41

WITHDRAWN
GLOBAL COOPERATION AFTER THE COLD WAR:
A REASSESSMENT OF TRILATERALISM

A Task Force Report to
The Trilateral Commission

Authors: JOSEPH S. NYE, JR.
Clarence Dillon Professor of International Affairs and
Director of the Center for International Affairs,
Harvard University

KURT BIEDENKOPF
Minister-President of the Free State of Saxony,
Germany

MOTOO SHIINA
President of the Policy Study Group;
former Member of the Japanese Diet

Special Consultant: BERNARD WOOD
Chief Executive Officer of the
Canadian Institute for International Peace and Security

published by
THE TRILATERAL COMMISSION
New York, Paris and Tokyo
July 1991

CARL A. RUDISILL LIBRARY
LENOIR-RHYNE COLLEGE

HF
1359
.N94
1991
Nov.1997

The Trilateral Commission was formed in 1973 by private citizens of Western Europe, Japan, and North America to foster closer cooperation among these three regions on common problems. It seeks to improve public understanding of such problems, to support proposals for handling them jointly, and to nurture habits and practices of working together among these regions.

© Copyright, 1991. The Trilateral Commission
All Rights Reserved.

Library of Congress Cataloging-in-Publication Data

Nye, Joseph S.
    Global cooperation after the Cold War: a reassessment of
trilateralism: a report to the Trilateral Commission/
authors, Joseph S. Nye, Jr., Kurt Biedenkopf, Motoo Shiina; special
consultant, Bernard Wood.
        p.   cm. — (The Triangle papers : 41)
    "March 1991."
    ISBN 0-930503-67-8 : $6.00
    1. International economic relations. 2. International cooperation.
3. International economic integration. I. Biedenkopf, Kurt H.
II. Shiina, Motoo, 1930–. III. Title. IV. Series.
HF1359.N94   1991   91-24370
337—dc20   CIP

Manufactured in the United States of America

THE TRILATERAL COMMISSION

345 East 46th Street   c/o Japan Center for   35, avenue de Friedland
New York, NY 10017   International Exchange   75008 Paris, France
                                    4-9-17 Minami-Azabu
                                    Minato-ku
                                    Tokyo, Japan

CARL A. RUDISILL LIBRARY

The Authors

JOSEPH S. NYE, JR. is Clarence Dillon Professor of International Affairs, Director of the Center for International Affairs and Associate Dean of Arts and Sciences at Harvard University. Educated at Princeton University (B.A., 1958), he did post-graduate work at Oxford University on a Rhodes Scholarship and earned a Ph.D. degree in political science from Harvard University, winning the Sumner Thesis Prize in 1964. From January 1977 to January 1979, he served as U.S. Deputy Under Secretary of State for Security Assistance, Science and Technology, and chaired the National Security Council Group on Non-Proliferation of Nuclear Weapons. Upon his departure, Secretary Vance awarded him the highest Department of State commendation, the Distinguished Honor Award. Professor Nye is a Senior Fellow of the Aspen Institute and Director of the Aspen Strategy Group. He is the American representative on the United Nations Advisory Committee on Disarmament Matters. A member of the editorial boards of *Foreign Policy* and *International Security*, he is also the author of numerous books and more than a hundred articles in professional journals. His most recent book is *Bound to Lead: The Changing Nature of American Power* (1990).

KURT BIEDENKOPF became Minister-President of the Free State of Saxony, Germany, in October 1990, and gave up his seat in the German Bundestag. Educated in economics and law in Germany and the United States, Dr. Biedenkopf taught at Frankfurt University (1963) and later at Ruhr University in Bochum, where he was Professor (1964–70) and President (1967–69). He was a member of the executive board of Henkel Corporation (1971–73) before becoming in 1973–77 Secretary General of the Christian Democratic Party (CDU). He also served the CDU as Deputy Chairman (1977–83) and, since 1983, as a member of the board. Dr. Biedenkopf was Chairman (and Co-Chairman) of the CDU in the State of Nordrhein-Westfalen (1977–87) and a member of the Landtag of Nordrhein-Westfalen (1980–83). He is a founder and board member of the Institute für Wirtschaft und Gesellschaft in Bonn and a guest professor at the Karl-Marx University in Leipzig (since January 1990). Dr. Biedenkopf is the author of numerous publications, including (most recently) *Die Neue Sicht der Dinge* (1985) and *Zeitsignale—Parteienlandschaft im Umbruch* (1989).

MOTOO SHIINA, former member of the Japanese Diet, is Founder and President of The Policy Study Group, a non-profit research group concerned with policy options. As a member of the Japanese Diet, he served in many capacities: Co-founder of the Diet Members' Council for Comprehensive Security (1980); Vice-Chairman of the LDP's Policy Research Council, responsible for national security, foreign affairs, and science and technology (1983–89); Director-General of the LDP International Bureau (1985–86); Member of the LDP Executive Council (1989–90); and Chairman of the Ethics Subcommittee of the Special Committee for Political Reform (1989–90). Since 1985, Mr. Shiina has been a member of the UK-Japan 2000 Group, and presently serves as the Chairman of the Japan side. Mr. Shiina was instrumental in establishing an institutional channel between Japanese Diet members and parliamentarians of NATO member countries. Educated in physics at Nagoya University, he worked as a nuclear reactor physicist with the Electric Power Development Company and, from 1959 to 1960, at the Argonne National Laboratory in the United States. In 1963, he established a company manufacturing automation components of which he is Chairman.

BERNARD WOOD (Special Consultant) is Chief Executive Officer of the Canadian Institute for International Peace and Security, a position he has held since February 1989. The Institute is a Crown Corporation established in 1984 to increase knowledge and understanding of issues relating to international peace and security from a Canadian perspective. Previously, Mr. Wood was the founding Director of the North-South Institute, an independent institute for research and information on international development, set up in 1976. Mr. Wood has held a series of special appointments. He was a Special Advisor to Canadian delegations to the UN General Assembly in 1979 and 1982. In the fall of 1985 and, again, in July 1986, Mr. Wood was the Personal-Representative of the Prime Minister of Canada to various Commonwealth heads of government in consultations on issues of Southern Africa. In 1989, he represented Canada on the seven-member Commonwealth observer mission to Namibia. Earlier in his career, Mr. Wood served with the Parliamentary Centre for Foreign Affairs in Ottawa, between 1973 and 1976 as Deputy Director. Mr. Wood was educated in Montreal, receiving his B.A. from Loyola College (now Concordia University) in 1966. He went on to complete an M.A. degree (international development specialization) at Carleton University's School of International Affairs in 1969.

The Trilateral Process

The report that follows is the joint responsibility of its authors. Joseph Nye assumed principal drafting responsibility for the opening and closing chapters, and for the U.S. section of the North American chapter. Motoo Shiina assumed primary responsibility for the Japan chapter, and Kurt Biedenkopf for the Europe chapter. Bernard Wood, a special consultant for this project, assumed primary responsibility for the Canada section of the North American chapter.

Although only the authors are responsible for the analysis and conclusions, they have been aided in their work by many others. Karl Kaiser was particularly helpful in the preparation of the Europe chapter. The persons consulted spoke for themselves as individuals and not as representatives of any institution with which they are associated. Those consulted or otherwise assisting in the development of the report include the following:

John Anderson, *Former Assistant Deputy Minister for Policy, Canadian Department of National Defense*

Narongchai Akrasanee, *Chairman of GF Group of Companies, Thailand; former Executive Vice President, Thai Development Research Institute*

Graham Allison, *Douglas Dillon Professor of Government, John F. Kennedy School of Government, Harvard University*

Edouard Balladur, *Member of the French National Assembly; former French Minister of Economy and Finance*

Howard Balloch, *Director-General, Policy Planning and Coodination, Canadian Department of External Affairs and International Trade*

Raymond Barre, *Member of National Assembly; former Prime Minister of France*

Robert L. Bartley, *Editor*, The Wall Street Journal

C. Fred Bergsten, *Director, Institute for International Economics; former U.S. Assistant Secretary of the Treasury for International Affairs*

Georges Berthoin, *European Chairman, The Trilateral Commission; International Honorary Chairman, European Movement*

Marcel Boiteux, *Honorary Chairman, French Electricity Board, Paris*

Gerald K. Bouey, *Former Governor, Bank of Canada*

James E. Burke, *Chairman of the Strategic Planning Committee, Johnson & Johnson*

Pierre Callebaut, *Chairman, Amylum, Brussels; former Chairman, Belgian Federation of Agricultural and Food Industries*

Hervé de Carmoy, *Chairman, Eresy; Advisor to the Chairman, HR Finances, Paris*

Jean-Claude Casanova, *Professor of Economics, Institute of Political Studies, Paris; Editor,* Commentaire

Gerald L. Curtis, *Professor of Political Science, East Asian Institute, Columbia University*

Lynn E. Davis, *Vice President and Director of the Arroyo Center, RAND Corporation*

Ian Deans, *Chairperson, Public Service Staff Relations Board of Canada*

Jean Deflassieux, *Chairman, Banque des Echanges Internationaux; Honorary Chairman, Crédit Lyonnais, Paris*

David B. Dewitt, *Director, Centre for International and Strategic Studies, York University*

Peter C. Dobell, *Director, Parliamentary Centre for Foreign Affairs and Foreign Trade, Ottawa*

Jessica Einhorn, *Director, Financial Operations Department, The World Bank*

René Foch, *Honorary General Director, Commission of the European Communities*

Andrew V. Frankel, *Assistant North American Director, The Trilateral Commission*

Richard N. Gardner, *Henry L. Moses Professor of Law and International Organization, Columbia University; of Counsel, Coudert Brothers; former U.S. Ambassador to Italy*

David Gergen, *Editor-at-Large,* U.S. News & World Report; *former U.S. Assistant to the President for Communications*

Pieter de Geus, *Former Vice Chairman, Netherlands Organization for Applied Scientific Research (TNO), The Hague; former Dutch Minister of Defense*

Allan E. Gotlieb, *Consultant, Stikeman-Elliott; former Canadian Ambassador to the United States*

Jacques Groothaert, *Chairman of the Board, Générale de Banque, Brussels; Honorary Ambassador of Belgium*

David G. Haglund, *Director, Centre for International Relations, Queen's University*

John Halstead, *Distinguished Research Professor, Georgetown University; former Canadian Ambassador to NATO*

Charles B. Heck, *North American Director, The Trilateral Commission*

Miguel Herrero de Miñon, *Member of the Spanish Parliament*

Jan Hinnekens, *Chairman, Belgian Boerenbond; Member, Board of Directors, National Bank of Belgium*

Richard C. Holbrooke, *Managing Director, Shearson Lehman Brothers, Inc.; former U.S. Assistant Secretary of State for East Asian and Pacific Affairs*

Bobby Ray Inman, *Chairman of the Executive Committee, Science Applications International Corporation; former Deputy Director, Central Intelligence Agency; former Director, National Security Agency*

Jacques Julliard, *Associate Director,* Le Nouvel Observateur, *Paris*

Karl Kaiser, *Director, Research Institute of the German Society for Foreign Affairs (D.G.A.P.), Bonn*

Christopher J. Kennan, *Associate to David Rockefeller*

Dorodjatun Kuntjoro-Jakti, *Director, Institute for Economic and Social Research, Faculty of Economics, University of Indonesia*

Lau Teik Soon, *Head, Department of Political Science, National University of Singapore; Member of Parliament*

Albert Legault, *Quebec Centre for International Relations, Laval University*

Pierre Lellouche, *Special Advisor to Jacques Chirac, Mayor of Paris*

Flora Lewis, *Senior Columnist,* The New York Times, *Paris*

Winston Lord, *former U.S. Ambassador to the People's Republic of China; former President, Council on Foreign Relations, New York; former Director of the Policy Planning Staff, U.S. Department of State*

Paul D. Manson, *Senior Vice President for Operations, Paramax Inc.; former Canadian Chief of the Defense Staff*

Paul Marantz, *Associate Professor of Political Science, University of British Columbia*

Caroline de Margerie, *Advisor (European Affairs), Presidency of the French Republic*

Gilles Martinet, *Ambassadeur de France; President, Association for the European Cultural Community, Paris*

Cesare Merlini, *Chairman, Institute for International Affairs, Rome*

Robert S. McNamara, *Former President, The World Bank; former U.S. Secretary of Defense*

Mark Moher, *Director-General, International Security, Arms Control and CSCE Affairs, Canadian Department of External Affairs and International Trade*

Pierre Morel, *Diplomatic Advisor to the President of the French Republic*

Alex Morrison, *Executive Director, Canadian Institute for Strategic Studies*

Charles Morrison, *Coordinator, International Relations Program, East-West Center, Honolulu; Senior Research Associate, Japan Center for International Exchange, Tokyo*

Jiro Murase, *Managing Partner, Marks Murase & White, New York*

Makito Noda, *Senior Program Officer, Japan Center for International Exchange, Tokyo*

Hisahiko Okazaki, *Japanese Ambassador to Thailand*

Sir Michael Palliser, *Deputy Chairman, Midland Bank; Chairman, Samuel Montagu & Co.; former Permanent Under-Secretary of State, Foreign and Commonwealth Office, London*

Paul Révay, *European Director, The Trilateral Commission*

Duff Roblin, *Member of the Canadian Senate*

David Rockefeller, *North American Chairman, The Trilateral Commission*

John E. Rielly, *President, Chicago Council on Foreign Relations*

John Roper, *Director, Institute for Security Studies, Western European Union; former Member of British Parliament*

François de Rose, *Ambassadeur de France; former Permanent Representative to NATO*

David A. Schatsky, *Paul Nitze School of Advanced International Studies, Johns Hopkins University*

François Scheer, *General Secretary, French Ministry of Foreign Affairs*

Hadi Soesastro, *Executive Director, Centre for Strategic and International Studies, Jakarta*

Denis Stairs, *Vice President, Dalhousie University*

Paula Stern, *President, The Stern Group, Washington, D.C.; former Chairwoman, U.S. International Trade Commission*

Mark S. Sternman, *School of International and Public Affairs, Columbia University*

Strobe Talbott, *Editor at Large and Foreign Affairs Columnist,* Time

Peter Tarnoff, *President, Council on Foreign Relations, New York*

Jacques Thierry, *Chairman of the Board, Banque Bruxelles Lambert; Chairman of the Board, Artois Piedboeuf Interbrew, Brussels*

Niels Thygesen, *Professor of Economics, Economics Institute, Copenhagen University*

Hubert Vedrine, *Presidential Spokesman and Special Advisor to the President of the French Republic (Strategic and Disarmament Issues)*

Simone Veil, *Member of European Parliament; former French Cabinet Minister; former President, European Parliament*

Will Wade-Gery, *Center for International Affairs, Harvard University*

Jusuf Wanandi, *Centre for Strategic and International Studies, Jakarta*

J.H. Warren, *North American Deputy Chairman, The Trilateral Commission; Principal Trade Policy Advisor, Government of Quebec; former Canadian Ambassador to the United States; former High Commissioner to the United Kingdom*

Karen Hastie Williams, *Partner, Crowell & Moring, Washington, D.C.*

Peter Witte, *The Trilateral Commission, New York*

Gerald Wright, *Senior Policy Advisor, Canadian Minister of State for Small Business and Tourism; former Advisor, Canadian Minister of Finance*

Somsakdi Xuto, *Professor, National Institute of Development Administration*
Tadashi Yamamoto, *Japanese Director, The Trilateral Commission*

SCHEDULE OF TASK FORCE ACTIVITIES:

May 1990 — Draft terms of reference prepared.

September 19 — British Group members discuss ideas for report, in London.

September 22-23 — Nye, Biedenkopf, Shiina and Wood meet at Harvard University to discuss chapter outlines and broad thrusts of report.

October 20 — European members, assembled in Venice for regional meeting, discuss ideas for report.

October 30 — Nye meets with current and former members in New York City to discuss ideas for report.

November 1-10 — Shiina discusses ideas for report with experts in Indonesia, Singapore and Thailand.

January 4, 1991 — Dutch Group members discuss ideas for report, in Amsterdam.

January 22 — Nye completes first draft of introductory chapter and U.S. section.

January 26 — First draft of Japan chapter completed.

January 29 — Nye meets, in Washington, D.C., with U.S. members to discuss main points in report.

February 3 — Nye and Biedenkopf meet in Munich to discuss report.

February 26 — Nye completes first draft of concluding chapter.

March 4 — Nye and Shiina meet at Harvard University to discuss report.

March 12 — Kaiser, on behalf of Biedenkopf, meets with Belgian members in Brussels.

March 15 — French Group members discuss ideas for report, in Paris.

March 19 — Kaiser, on behalf of Biedenkopf, meets with French members, political leaders and government officials in Paris.

Late March — Tokyo meeting draft completed for circulation to Trilateral Commission members. Draft Europe chapter completed in mid-April.

April 20-22 — Draft report discussed in Tokyo at annual meeting of Trilateral Commission.

June — Final revisions completed.

Summary of Report

Some observers believe the 1990s will see "three-blocism." The United States will concentrate on North America and the Western Hemisphere; Japan will form the heart of a yen bloc in East Asia; and the European Community will be the center of a larger self-sustained European region. The conditions of the 1990s, it is argued, will make it impossible for broad multilateral cooperation—a public good of which the three main democratic industrialized areas of the world have been the primary trustees—to continue.

With the end of the Cold War, centrifugal forces among the Trilateral countries are likely to increase. The decline of Soviet power and the diminished appeal of Communist ideology have removed the overarching common threat that was clear to public opinion in the Trilateral democracies.

During the Cold War, the need to present a common front in the face of the common external threat helped to dampen economic conflicts or at least to keep them in proportion. Now, interdependence continues to grow but the security blanket has been removed.

In addition, with the absence of an external threat, the 1990s will see increased internal preoccupation within the Trilateral regions. Europe will be intensely preoccupied with its own integration as well as its relations with its neighbors. The United States may turn inward to a domestic agenda of reform. Canada is grappling with fundamental issues of national unity. Finally Japan, if rebuffed by Europe and the United States, may halt its first steps toward a greater global role in favor of a more regional orientation.

The separate blocs vision of the world has a number of problems, however. For one thing, the trends in technology and economics run against a bloc view. Thus some political and economic forces will resist fragmentation of the international economy. Second, the idea of separate blocs runs counter to the nationalism in many non-Trilateral countries concerned about a large Trilateral neighbor and about maintaining an open international economy that provides access outside the region. These countries may develop an interest in Trilateral cooperation rather than separate blocs.

Finally, the three-bloc view runs counter to the fact that, even after the Cold War, America remains important to the security of both Europe and East Asia. So long as residual concerns remain about the outcome of the second Russian Revolution and the potential threat which the Soviet Union can pose to Western Europe, an American security guarantee remains valuable. Similarly, so long as Japan retains its peace constitution yet lives in a region where other states, particularly China and the Soviet Union, retain nuclear weapons, an American security guarantee remains an important part of the geopolitical stability of that region as well.

Another argument used in support of the view that Trilateral cooperation, and thus broad global cooperation, will not continue relates to the turmoil associated with the rise or fall of great powers—in particular the presumed decline of the United States. But this decline is greatly exaggerated. The American share of world product has held steady at roughly the same level of 23 percent from 1974 to 1990, after the wearing off of the "World War II effect" that meant an abnormally high U.S. share in earlier postwar years. When the Trilateral Commission was formed in the early 1970s, North America, the European Community, and Japan represented about 60 percent of the world economy. They still do today.

The problems of the 1990s are to be understood less in terms of the rise or fall of great powers than in terms of the "diffusion of power." With the growth of economic interdependence, the proliferation of transnational actors, nationalism in weak states, the spread of technology, and the increasing number of issues which are both domestic and international, all great powers will be less able to use their traditional power resources to achieve their purposes. Since most of the resulting issues cannot be managed unilaterally, states will have a strong incentive to develop international cooperation. In sum, the need for Trilateral cooperation in a wider global context is as great, perhaps greater than ever.

One of the problems of cooperation in the post-Cold War period will be finding ways to dramatize the benefits of cooperation, to represent the long-run self-interest of countries, and to escape the veto power of particular groups. Can political leaders who understand the challenges make the arguments for international cooperation more persuasive than the alternatives to public opinion in the Trilateral democracies?

An agenda for broad multilateral cooperation is critical for dramatizing the benefits of cooperation, and the concluding chapter of this report is largely devoted to setting forth such an agenda. The agenda ranges from substantive global problems (sustainable global economic growth and development, peaceful change in the declining Soviet empire, non-proliferation of advanced weapons technology, means to address transnational global issues), to strengthening the global roles of Japan and a more integrated European Community, to key aspects of process (more attention to international institutions, greater decision-sharing and burden-sharing). In the setting of the 1990s, groups favoring cooperation will need to reinforce each other by forming coalitions across national borders. The Trilateral Commission will need to think of itself as helping to formulate transnational coalitions that advance the common good.

Table of Contents

I. Introduction

Our planet's politics bear an odd resemblance to its geology. For long periods of time, the great tectonic plates seem so stable that we take order for granted. But underneath the surface, tensions build and eventually we experience earthquakes—or revolutions. For four decades from the late 1940s, world order rested on a seemingly stable bipolar structure. However, economic and political strains were building beneath the surface. Earthquakes were felt with the Eastern European revolutions of 1989. Iraq's invasion of Kuwait in 1990 was another significant shake. It is unlikely that all the tremors are over. The second Russian Revolution is still in its early stages. The decline in Soviet power has been accompanied by the increasing economic integration of Europe and the continuing rise of Japanese economic power. The shape of a "new world order" remains open and fluid.

Given the upheavals in world politics, a reassessment of Trilateral cooperation, indeed of the Trilateral Commission, is timely. Is Trilateral cooperation still relevant in this new era? Are the three main democratic industrialized centers of the postwar international system going to work together or split apart?

The Original Trilateral Concept

One basic idea propelling the creation of the Trilateral Commission in the early 1970s was a sense that the United States was no longer (and would not again be) in such a singularly dominant position in the management of the international system. A more shared form of leadership—centered on the "Trilateral" areas—would be required to steer the international system through the challenges that lay ahead.

Another basic idea was a sense that issues of global economic interdependence were rising in importance on the policy agenda alongside more classical political-security issues, and needed to be so recognized. Growing economic interdependence produced benefits but also frictions, as was seen in the disputes over trade and monetary arrangements in the early 1970s. The "oil shock" in the fall of 1973, and demands for a "new international economic order" that would interfere with world markets, added to the sense of global challenge.

The immediate context of East-West relations in the early 1970s was one of "detente" with the Soviet Union and a major positive shift in relations with China. Nevertheless, there remained a sense of historical competition with the Soviet Union and of ideological competition with Communism. Some in our own countries wondered about the long-term future of democratic institutions. As late as 1976, Leonid Brezhnev told a major Western leader that Communism would dominate the world by 1995.

In these circumstances, the founders of the Commission sought to draw together the highest-level private group possible from the three core democratic industrialized areas of the world. The Trilateral Commission helped to bring Japan more fully into the international concert, and to support global leadership perspectives in Western Europe and North America. Trilateral discussion reinforced commitment to a community of democratic values, helped to maintain an open market approach toward the international economy, and reinforced concerns for dealing with the poorer parts of the globe. Whatever the causes, many recent trends have been favorable for these endeavors of Trilateral cooperation.

Some might grant that the Trilateral Commission made a modest contribution to dealing with the problems identified in the early 1970s, but nevertheless contend that the world of the 1990s will be too different to sustain Trilateral cooperation. The most obvious change is the end of the Cold War—the removal of our "image of an enemy" as one Soviet academician put it—and the decline of Soviet power. Even if the Soviet Union turns in more harsh directions internally and externally, it will not pose the same threat it did in the past half century. Loss of the Soviet empire and the demise of the Warsaw Pact in Eastern Europe means that the danger of an invasion of Europe without adequate warning is greatly diminished. Moreover, a return to repression and centralization at home would not reverse but accelerate long-term Soviet decline based on the inability of the centralized planning system to come to terms with the third industrial revolution, i.e., the development of an information-based economy.

For most of the Cold War, the economic conflicts that accompanied growing interdependence among the Trilateral countries occurred under the cover of an overall security blanket. The need to present a common front in the face of a common external threat helped to dampen economic conflicts or at least to keep them in proportion. Now, interdependence continues to grow but the security blanket has been removed. Moreover, even as interdependence produces benefits, it also stimulates fears as traditional or protected positions are shaken. Thus at the same time that trends in technology and economics are increasing the globalization of communications and corporate strategy, they are also accentuating nationalism in the responses of those who are less mobile. The dramatic and generally beneficial growth of the East Asian economies, for instance, is seen as a threat to jobs and national identity by significant sectors of the public in North America and in Europe. At the same time, protected sectors of the Japanese economy remain reluctant to accept painful changes associated with international interdependence.

In addition, with the absence of an external threat, the 1990s will see increased internal preoccupation in the Trilateral regions. For example, while German unification is a great gain for democracy, it also means that Europe will be intensely preoccupied with its own integration as well as its relations with its stable neighbors in the European Free Trade Association and its less stable neighbors to the east. At the same time, the United States, which historically has gone through cycles of inward and outward attention, may turn inward to a domestic agenda of reform. Education, urban improvement, racial progress, and absorbing immigrants may take precedence over international issues. Canada is grappling with fundamental issues of national unity. And finally Japan, if rebuffed by Europe and the United States, may halt its first steps toward a greater global role in favor of a more regional orientation.

Throughout history, the rapid rise and fall of great powers has created wakes of turmoil. The 1990s is likely to see the continued rapid rise of Japan as a global economic power, the consolidation of Europe as an economic power, and the decline of the Soviet Union. In such circumstances, it is argued, the prospects for conflict will increase and Trilateral cooperation will become more problematic. Some observers believe that whatever the merits of Trilateralism as an approach to the problems identified in the 1970s, the conditions of the 1990s will make it impossible to continue. Rather than Trilateralism, the 1990s will see "three-blocism." The United States will concentrate on North America and the Western Hemisphere; Japan will form the heart of a yen bloc in East Asia; and Europe will be the center of a larger self-sustained European region with Africa as an appendage. Alternatively, given Europe's internal preoccupation, the world may divide into two large blocs, one based in Europe and the other around the Pacific Basin. Reality will probably fall somewhere between these visions of full Trilateral cooperation and separate blocs, but many observers see the outcome closer to the separate blocs end of the spectrum.

The Case for Continuing Trilateralism

This pessimistic scenario cannot be dismissed lightly. With the end of the Cold War, centrifugal forces among the Trilateral countries are likely to increase. The Trilateral coalition would not be the first coalition to fall apart after a major victory. Cooperation is becoming more difficult in a post-Cold War world.

However, not all trends are discouraging for Trilateral cooperation. For example, there are more similarities between the early 1970s and the early 1990s than the pessimists admit. As noted above, when the Commission was formed in the early 1970s, "detente" had somewhat diminished the sense of Soviet threat, and there was widespread belief in the decreasing role of military power in world politics. In addition, there was increasing attention to interdependence, both to the frictions generated by economic interdependence and the anxieties arising from a new awareness of environmental interdependence. Concerns about U.S. isolationism, European parochialism, and Japan's willingness to develop an international role characterized that period as much as the current one.

The mid-1970s marked the end of three decades of American decline from the abnormally high share of world product achieved at the end of World War II, back to more normal proportions on the eve of the Second World War. The recovery and growth of Europe and Japan, a process aided and abetted by America's global strategy of containment and maintaining an open international economy, meant that the American share of world product declined from nearly half of the world total at the end of the Second World War to some 23 percent of the total by 1974. This adjustment to a diminished U.S. role in the world in the early 1970s was symbolized by the withdrawal from Vietnam in the security area and the closing of the "gold window" (i.e., ending the convertibility of the dollar into gold) in the economic area. Contrary to prevalent opinion, however, the American share of world product has held steady at roughly the same level of 23 percent from 1974 to 1990.

When the Trilateral Commission was formed in the early 1970s, North America, the European Community, and Japan represented about 60 percent of the world economy. As the following table shows, they still do so today. Although a minority of the world's population, the Trilateral countries remain the leading trustees of the world economy.

TABLE 1
Shares of World Product
(percent)

	1970	1989
United States and Canada	28.8	28.3
European Community (12)	23.8	21.7
Japan	7.5	9.5
Rest of the World	39.9	40.5
Total	100.0	100.0

Source: Central Intelligence Agency, *Handbook of Economic Statistics, 1990*
Note: GNP figures have been converted to a common unit using OECD purchasing-
power-parity exchange rates.

The separate blocs vision of the world is not without problems. For one thing, the trends in technology and economics run against a bloc view. While some corporations will be satisfied with protected niches, others wishing to achieve economies of scale in Trilateral markets will not want to be limited to one third of the potential market. In that sense, some strong economic and political forces will resist fragmentation of the international economy. Second, the idea of separate blocs runs counter to the nationalism in many of the countries lumped together. For example, Latin Americans do not want to become solely dependent on the United States, Asians do not want to be limited to a yen bloc, nor do Africans or East Europeans want to be mere appendages of Western Europe. For those who are concerned about their neighbors, maintaining an open global economy with access to those outside the region will remain important in the 1990s. In that regard, other parts of the world may develop an interest in Trilateral cooperation rather than separate blocs.

Finally, the three-bloc view runs counter to the fact that, even after the Cold War, America remains important to the security of both Europe and East Asia. So long as residual concerns remain about the outcome of the second Russian Revolution and the potential threat which the Soviet Union (or Russia) can pose to Western Europe, an American security guarantee remains valuable. Similarly, so long as Japan retains its peace constitution yet lives in a region where other states, particularly China and the Soviet Union, retain nuclear weapons, an American security guarantee remains an important part of the geopolitical stability of that region as well. But it is hard to imagine the security guarantees retaining their credibility if the world economy degenerates into trade wars and isolated trading regions. The demand for common security, even if less intense than during the Cold War, may still serve to dampen some of the economic conflicts.

Rather than the traditional rise and fall of great powers with its attendant turmoil, the 1990s may see a different problem—the continued diffusion of power. All great powers will be less able to use their traditional power resources to achieve their purposes than in the past. On many issues, private actors and small states will become more powerful. At least five factors contribute to this diffusion of power: economic interdependence, transnational actors, nationalism in weak states, the spread of technology, and the increasing number of issues which are both domestic and international. Since most of the resulting issues cannot be managed unilaterally, states have a strong incentive to develop international cooperation. In that sense, some of the conditions of the 1990s may foster a climate for new aspects of Trilateral cooperation.

In other words, the 1990s will differ from earlier periods of Trilateralism because of the absence of the overarching security concern presented by the Soviet Union during the Cold War. But in many other areas, especially in the growth of economic interdependence and the rise of transnational issues, trends in the 1990s recall the early days of Trilateralism. Furthermore, dealing successfully with the new challenges discussed below seems less likely either unilaterally or within a single region than through continued international and Trilateral cooperation.

Thus the end of the Cold War does not mean the end of the need for Trilateral cooperation, although it does make maintaining cooperation among the leading democracies more difficult. The unifying perception, the common thread of a single overarching security threat, has been replaced by the challenges represented by the diffusion of power. However, the need for Trilateral cooperation is as great, perhaps greater than ever. The key question is whether the political leaders who understand those challenges can make the arguments for international cooperation more persuasive than the alternatives to the publics in the Trilateral democracies.

In the final chapter of this report we set out a ten-point agenda for Trilateral cooperation in the 1990s. The political setting in each region is examined in more detail in the three chapters that immediately follow.

II. NORTH AMERICA AND TRILATERAL COOPERATION

THE UNITED STATES

For 40 years, American strategy was largely defined by the perception of Soviet threat. Now the Soviet Union is unquestionably in decline and Americans are debating their future role in the world. Victory in the Cold War was followed not by a mood of triumphalism, but one of unease. Before the Gulf War, polls showed half the American public believing the country was in decline. A rash of books and articles were published about the decline of nations in general, and the position of the United States in particular. "Declinists" see the United States, like previous empires, in a long-term decline. They see the events in the Persian Gulf as merely a temporary interruption. "Revivalists" argue that while the country has serious problems, it is still capable of mastering them.

Declinists and revivalists agree that the United States is less powerful now than it was at mid-century. Even conservative estimates show that the U.S. share of global product declined from more than a third of the total in 1950 to a less than a fourth in the 1980s. However, one must take into account the "World War II effect." Unlike others, the United States (and Canada as well) was *strengthened* by the war. The relative decline from 1945 to 1975 was simply a return to normal after the artificial effects of World War II. As noted above, the American share of world product held constant at 23 percent after the mid-1970s. The American share of the total product of the major industrial democracies actually increased slightly in the 1980s.

In assessing the change in American power, one must also beware of the "golden glow of the past." If one exaggerates the extent to which the United States dominated in the past, one is bound to feel diminished in the present. Even at the peak of its power, the United States was not able to prevent the Soviet Union or France from developing nuclear weapons, nor could it prevent the "loss" of China, Cuba, or Vietnam. The United States was never such an imperial colossus.

Similar problems plague efforts to measure and evaluate the serious social problems in the United States such as drug use, violence, racism, family stability, and the fact that a quarter of the population does not complete secondary school. Some of these problems, such as drug use, are worse today than 30 years ago. Others, such as racism or the position of women in society, are somewhat better than 30 years ago. Still others are hard to evaluate. For example, high-school completion rates are higher than 30 years ago, but much lower than Japan's 95 percent, and the performance is inadequate for the needs of an information-based economy. What is clear is that if one compares only the bad in the present with the good in the past, it is easy to show decline. Problems have to be dealt with on their own merits.

The United States also has economic problems. Important industrial sectors such as consumer electronics and automobiles have slipped badly. The household savings rate dropped from 8 percent in the 1970s to 5 percent in the late 1980s. In addition, the government's deficit contributed another 3 percent drop in net savings. Since gross investment stayed roughly the same, the missing savings were made up by capital imports that transformed the United States into the world's largest debtor nation in absolute terms. In the 1990s, if the U.S. savings rate remains low and it becomes more difficult to attract foreign capital, investment rates will suffer with attendant negative effects on productivity and growth.

Again, if one looks only at the negative side of the ledger, the situation seems glum. But there is another side of the story. During the 1980s, the American economy grew by 2.5 percent a year, a rate above its historical average of 2 percent per annum over the past century. Contrary to the view that the United States is becoming "de-industrialized," manufacturing contributed the same roughly one fifth of Gross National Product that it did in the 1970s. In fact, the share of manufacturing increased slightly in the 1980s. Moreover, productivity in manufacturing rose by 3.5 percent per year in the 1980s, and absolute productivity (product per worker) remained higher than in Japan or Germany. In other words, it is a mistake to generalize from autos or consumer electronics to all industry. The United States continues in the forefront of industries like aircraft, chemicals, biotechnology, or computers. Moreover, some economists believe that the slow 1 percent rate of growth of overall labor productivity (i.e., in all sectors) is an underestimate that reflects the difficulty of measuring productivity increases in the service sector.

In short, the United States has serious domestic problems, particularly improving education and savings which underlie investment and future gains in productivity. In addition, there are serious social problems related to poverty, race, and the condition of inner cities. Unless these problems are addressed, the future will be diminished. In a world of transnational interdependence, effective international measures start at home. Thus a precondition for Trilateral cooperation is for the United States to get its domestic house in order. Just as it was a mistake for Americans to exaggerate their weakness before the Gulf War, it would be a mistake to exaggerate their strengths after the War. Moreover, the international problems that confront the United States stem less from decline than from the growth of interdependence and the diffusion of power. The United States is more intertwined with the rest of the world. For example, exports plus imports of goods and services now represent about 21 percent of GNP, which is almost double the level of twenty years ago. But historical analogies portraying Americans in some inexorable decline are misleading and may, in turn, stimulate inward-turning or protectionist reactions. Choices are still open.

American Strategic Choices
The shape of the post-Cold War world will depend in part on American strategic choices. If the United States neglects its alliances, Japanese and European fears will increase. Moreover, as interdependence and the diffusion of power to non-state actors and small states grow, the implications for stability and welfare will depend heavily on whether the largest state takes a lead in organizing international order.

After the Gulf War, some observers see the United States as the only superpower and fear American efforts at hegemony. But such fears fail to take into account the economic multipolarity of the world or the general diffusion of power on issues relating to interdependence. Moreover, there is little inclination toward hegemony in American public opinion. In fact, not all Americans agree that U.S. leadership is important. Without the galvanizing challenge of a totalitarian threat such as Fascism or Communism, some observers argue for more attention at home and less abroad. Throughout its history, American foreign policy has been marked by cycles of inward and outward orientation. With 30 percent of its resources going to government, the United States is more lightly taxed than other Trilateral countries and can afford both domestic and international security, particularly since the military burdens should be lighter in a post-Cold War world. Some retrenchment from past high levels is still consistent with a major international role. But why, many Americans ask, should we still worry about leadership?

The simplest answer is in the new dimensions of interdependence. Drawing back from current international commitments will not stop technological change, or the development and global extension of an information-based economy, or a high degree of dependence upon transnational actors. Terrorism, drug traffic, AIDS, and global warming will intrude upon Americans whether they like it or not. Nor are there purely domestic solutions to such transnational problems. Absence of leadership by the largest country would reduce the ability of all states to deal with such problems of interdependence. Managing interdependence is a major reason for investing American resources for international leadership and must be central to a new strategy.

There are also traditional geopolitical problems which if ignored could create security problems that could come to haunt the United States. The lessons from earlier periods indicate that if the strongest state does not lead, the prospects for instability increase. The Cold War may be over, but the reduced role of ideology does not mean the end of history, nor does it allow states to be indifferent to the balance of power.

The United States still has a continuing interest in European security for several reasons. Because Soviet (or Russian) intentions could change, the mere existence of such impressive and proximate military capabilities cannot be ignored. Declining empires have lashed out before. Second, the American security presence, even at greatly reduced troop levels, has a reassuring effect as European integration proceeds. Finally, the situation in Eastern Europe could become politically disruptive as some of those economically weak nations move toward greater national assertiveness. The United States has an interest in a secure and prosperous Western Europe that gradually draws the Eastern European economies and societies toward pluralism and democracy. The primary role will rest with the Europeans, but if the United States were to divorce itself from the process, it might find the future geopolitical situation far less stable.

The United States also has geopolitical interests and a major role in the Pacific. At this point, the United States is the only country with both economic and military power resources in the region. Other Asian powers desire a continued American security presence because they do not want Japan to feel compelled to remilitarize. The domestic political consensus in Japan is currently opposed to such a military build-up. The United States' interest in the stability of the Asian balance, and in obtaining Japanese help on transnational issues, is best served by continuing its alliance and security presence in the region.

U.S.-Japan Relations

Some Americans disagree with this view of U.S. interests. Public opinion polls show that many Americans fear that Japan will replace the Soviet Union as the primary challenger in the post-Cold War era. Some even go so far as to predict eventual military conflict. Such views are too alarmist. One should not leap too quickly to the conclusion that all trends favor Japan. For example, in a situation of interdependence, the very size and diversity of the United States makes it relatively less dependent. Thus, if the United States borrows from Japan, Japan gains influence but it also develops a stake in the health of the U.S. economy. If Japan then refused to lend to the United States, it would diminish the value of its existing investments and might risk its access to the large American market, which it needs more than America needs the Japanese market.

The ability to influence others is often associated with the possession of certain resources such as population, territory, natural resources, economic resources (capital, labor, technology), military forces, and political stability. These might be considered the portfolio of resources that produce power in international politics. While economic power may be a more important part of the portfolio than in previous eras, the other dimensions remain important, including military power. In that sense, the United States has a more diversified power portfolio than Japan. Moreover, the United States is well-endowed with "soft power"— i.e., the ability to attract others to do what it wishes—enhanced by a universalistic culture and a major role in international institutions. Fears that Japan will replace the United States or challenge it for the "number one" position in the 1990s are greatly exaggerated and rest on a truncated view of power in international politics. A little more self-confidence and less anxiety on the part of Americans about the rise of Japanese power would make U.S.-Japan cooperation on the many issues of common transnational concern a great deal easier.

Even so, it would be a mistake to deny that there will be important problems in U.S.-Japan relations. As the two societies become more interdependent, policy differences will have a stronger effect. For instance, Americans complain about mercantilist government policies as well as cultural and business practices which make the Japanese market less accessible to American companies than the American market is to Japanese companies. Similarly, patterns of ownership make it far easier for a Japanese company to invest in the United States than for its American competitor to invest in Japan. This asymmetry gives rise to attitudes of resentment about the Japanese not playing fair in the situation of economic interdependence; this in turn feeds policies of protectionism as well as crude nationalistic responses. There are always enough anecdotes and real incidents to provide fuel for these political fires.

One response has been to press Japan to open its markets. This outside pressure has often accomplished market-opening but also leads to resentment and nationalism in Japan. In some instances, such as the Structural Impediments Initiative of 1989-90, U.S. and Japanese negotiators discussed policies that were traditionally deep within the domestic jurisdiction of each other's government. Ironically, since many of the changes that U.S. negotiators pressed for are in the interests of Japanese consumers and vice versa, certain transnational alliances were formed which may have made both countries better off. But other issues were highly sensitive and stimulated nationalistic responses.

Another school of thought, sometimes called the "revisionist" school, argues that Japan is not likely to change or at least not change quickly. In this view, the United States should not try to open Japanese markets because that requires going deeply into Japanese culture and society and is bound to create deep resentments. Instead the United States should permit Japanese sales to U.S. markets in proportion to the extent that American products are imported into Japan. Similarly, Japanese direct investment in the United States (which is four times U.S. direct investment in Japan) might be similarly limited until the proportions are similar. Such an approach, sometimes called "containing Japan" or managing U.S.-Japanese trade and investment on a reciprocal basis, would have the effect of closing certain American markets to Japan. Proponents argue that this approach is more respectful of Japanese culture and independence than is the traditional market-opening approach, and they argue that it will be better for U.S.-Japan relations in the long run.

Thus far the market-opening approach has been the dominant approach in the United States but the "revisionist" view has some strong support in public opinion, in the Congress, and among a number of intellectuals. The debate between the different approaches to managing U.S.-Japan economic relations will be strongly affected by the ability of the Japanese government and society to speed up the current slow pace of change in Japan. The implementation of the Structural Impediments Initiative will be closely watched by both sides. Moreover, as Japanese investment increases in the United States and Japanese subsidiaries begin to act more like American firms, the question arises whether American interests in terms of the quality of jobs and employment opportunities for Americans are better served by Japanese firms in the United States or American firms working overseas. In short, in a world of increasing interdependence, the question of "Who is us?" is less easily answered.

U.S.-European Relations

The United States has been strongly supportive of European integration throughout the postwar period. Indeed, early in the postwar period, the United States accepted discrimination against American goods for the sake of encouraging a stronger and more integrated Europe, for a strong Europe was seen as a bulwark against Communism and the encroachment of Soviet power. Economic disputes, of which there have been many going back to the famous "chicken war" in the 1960s, were generally kept under control because of overarching security concerns. There were many points of consultation between the United States and Europe, and the NATO structure in particular led to a constant and intimate interaction under American leadership. Now with the Cold War threat removed, NATO plays a somewhat less central role and the European Community has become the dominant institution in Europe. The United States remains sympathetic and supportive toward European integration, although there have been frequent complaints about European tendencies to resolve internal difficulties among the twelve member-states without adequate consultation with the United States and sometimes at the expense of American economic interests. The setback in the GATT talks in December 1990 further shook the U.S.-European relationship.

The American government has suggested a number of times the desirability of better communications between the European Community and the United States, but has been resisted on the grounds that the Americans do not deserve the thirteenth seat at the European table. In the meantime, the fact that more issues are dealt with by trade and functional ministries and that fewer of these issues appear on the agendas of top political leaders means that the prospects for friction seem to be increasing. Moreover, even with good will, the preoccupation of Europeans with the difficult task of consolidating the unification of Germany, perfecting the Community of the Twelve, and gradually integrating the "concentric circles" of European neighbors into a viable larger Community pushes American concerns to the back burner. This, in turn, fans resentment in Congress, which then tends to revive the issue of burden-sharing in the security area as well. The fact that the United States provided such a large share of the troops in the Gulf War was cited by some in Congress as an example of Europeans failing to pay their fair share, although the performance of British, French, and Italian forces, and the increased German financial contribution, somewhat alleviated the problem. Europeans, on the other hand, argue that they do not wish to be a tail on an American dog wagged by American conceptions of their interest in the Middle East. They complained that Americans failed to consult adequately with them and then expected them to take part. Similar complaints are heard in the American-Japanese relationship.

Americans complain about their Trilateral partners having a free ride, but nevertheless this leaves Americans steering the bus. Conversely, if Americans want the others to pay full freight, they will have to be more alert to the problems of discussion and consultation about who will drive and what paths or roads will be taken. Americans show considerable ambivalence about their leadership role. They want others to pay, but are not in the habit of giving them an effective say. The experience in the Gulf, with its preponderant American military role, did little to change these habits. Americans will have to learn that their influence in the post-Cold War world rests on their "soft power" as exemplified by their ability to form voluntary coalitions, as well as on their "hard" economic and military power. But effectiveness in forming such coalitions will require improved habits of consultation. In other words, even if maintaining the Trilateral alliances makes good sense in both security and economic terms, cooperation among the Trilateral democracies in the absence of an overriding common threat will not be easy.

CANADA

Canadian perspectives on the future of cooperation among the Trilateral regions are of particular interest for three reasons. First, as a middle-sized country with stakes in the Trilateral grouping and in many broader associations, the outlook from Canada may have some wider relevance, especially to other middle and smaller powers.

Second, the possibility that Trilateral cooperation and multilateral regimes will be supplanted by a system of regional blocs would have particular and pronounced implications for Canada. Third, Canada exhibits rather starkly the prevalent tension between forces of globalization (and integration) on the one hand, and ethnic and sub-national assertion (or disintegration) on the other, without an intermediate political framework like that provided by the European Community for its member-countries with similar internal tensions.

Canada and a "New World Order"

The Cold War order as such is clearly dead, but the shape of its successor order is far from clear; and Canadians know, as one of the most "international" of nations, that their lives and institutions will be influenced in this transition. While political and economic competition between the superpowers has largely dissipated, Canada's territory and air space remain uncomfortably placed between the remaining—and still-developing—Soviet and American nuclear arsenals. There are no multilateral security mechanisms—comparable to those of the new Europe—on its Pacific flank. On the Atlantic side, Canada is committed to the new CSCE mechanisms and to the remaining North Atlantic security guarantees, both of which will require new definition and creativity in the dynamic and difficult European environment now emerging.

As one of the Trilateral countries most unwaveringly committed to the United Nations, Canada was solidly supportive when the Iraqi aggression against Kuwait called forth the political, economic and military response envisaged when the United Nations was founded, but Canadians share the concern of many others that the world does not have in place the accompanying arrangements for the satisfactory sharing of military burdens and decisions. Consistent standards of order, and their consistent application, will also be essential in the future if credibility is to be maintained.

The shape of the new world order that will now emerge, and the allocation of responsibilities for its maintenance, are of strong interest to Canada for both their direct and systemic implications.

Canada has as strong a direct stake as any other outside country in the ways in which the United States will perceive and pursue its changing leadership responsibilities in the post-Cold War order, and in the ways in which others will share the burdens. An over-extended United States, or one resentful of the distribution of the responsibilities and benefits of international order—particularly with

Europe and Japan—would present many problems for Canada.

With strong family links in parts of the Soviet Union and Eastern and Central Europe, Canadians share fully in the celebration of the embryonic growth of democratic values in that region and the moves toward market economies. In spite of geographical distance, therefore, Canada wishes to contribute, in the complementary ways that outsiders can, to help these agonizing transitions to succeed. Canadians will support steps to integrate these countries, as quickly as they are ready, into international institutions and normal international relationships.

Attentive Canadians understand that the current GATT Round represents a crossroads for the international economy: what is at stake now is not simply the pace and cost of liberalization and adjustment among Trilateral countries, but the very integrity of the non-discriminatory system, and the legitimacy and utility of the GATT principles for the wider world which has just come to embrace them. Blatantly discriminatory standards and a glacial pace in attacking profound and damaging anomalies such as agricultural trade barriers and unsatisfactory trade rules could seriously undermine the worldwide movement toward acceptance of rational economic strategies. Canada's bilateral Free Trade Agreement with the United States and the projected three-way agreements with Mexico are supported as being consistent with GATT obligations and as steps toward wider multilateral liberalization.

Canada's direct stakes blend into its stake in the international system itself, and into its potential for creative contributions to the management of the Trilateral countries' relations with others in the new approaches to multilateral cooperation that may now become possible. For almost half a century, Canadian foreign policy has explicitly recognized and consistently pursued multilateral cooperation as a central strategy for "middle" and smaller powers. This general approach has been more or less successful, depending on the issue-area and the prevailing circumstances. The UN's peace and security functions have until recently been the central disappointment, but even there Canada was able to play a pivotal part in the "fallback" response of peacekeeping.

In the wake of the Cold War and under the demands of interdependence, multilateral cooperation clearly has a new chance, and the time may also have come for wider acceptance of two related approaches long favored by Canada. One is the encouragement of "functionalism," i.e., that functional, transnational links between societies, firms and citizens be allowed to grow with the minimum of politicization and government interference. The second is the "functional principle of representation," under which states assume decision-making responsibility and cost burdens in particular arenas of international relations commensurate with their stakes and influence in those arenas. As a general response to the perennial problems of "burden-sharing" and "free riders", this approach may now have a good deal to offer. It may also call for some revision of the current structures of "permanent membership," vetoes and weighted voting in international institutions to ensure a proper balance between influence, representation and responsibility.

Canada still seems to be well-placed to play certain useful "bridging" roles in this changing international environment, both within and beyond the Trilateral regions. Among the Trilateral countries there is continuing, and in some ways increased, value in Canada's Atlantic participation as "the other North American" in NATO and CSCE activities, while Canada's Pacific identity and interests are being asserted more vigorously, by business groups, governments and others, with the implication that Canada will be prepared to accept greater responsibilities in that region. In the Third World, Canada's non-imperial record, its Commonwealth, Francophone, inter-American and Pacific links, its relatively generous aid programs, and its unparalleled peacekeeping roles, all provide firm foundations for attempts to forge better working links beyond the Trilateral group. For the large and growing majority of humanity in the "developing" countries of Asia, Africa and Latin America, there is already a widespread fear that improved East-West relations will increase their own marginalization and deprivation. This will be their test of the legitimacy and sustainability of any "new world order," and much will hang on the outcome: from the proliferation of security threats, to the management of migration pressures and environmental sustainability.

The Constitutional Crisis and the International Context

The powerful effects of international change on economic and political interests in Canada—in trade policy decisions, for instance—are especially thorny and vulnerable to abuse when they parallel the political fault lines of constitutional tension. One such rift is found in the different trade interests and approaches between Prairie grain producers and the supply-managed agricultural sectors which dominate in Quebec and other parts of Central Canada. This phenomenon is neither new nor unique to Canada, and traditionally the pressures of international codes and reciprocal bargaining have helped governments to adopt more efficient and rational practices. Internally, Canada's innovation of "regional equalization" and strong, standardized social safety nets have helped to ease and buffer the differential impacts.

Many Canadians doubt that these internal mechanisms can continue to function with the possible devolution of further economic and social jurisdictions to the provinces, and some doubt that they can continue to be adequately financed in any case in more competitive North American and global environments. Canada's capacity to adjust to current international economic conditions and adapt itself for the future is already severely constrained by huge public sector debts and continuing budget deficits, in spite of substantial efforts at economic policy rationalization in coordination with agreed G-7 goals. With globalization likely to affect adversely some sectors of the Canadian economy, a continued incapacity to pursue concerted national strategies in education, training, research and development is likely to lead to decline in the country's international economic weight.

International bargaining power will also be affected. If the new constitutional arrangements which will now come in Canada produce much more decentralized control over economic and foreign policy, the overall strength and efficacy of Canadians' international action will unquestionably be diminished. An Ottawa drained of its powers to "deliver" internationally could bring little of use to discussions of Trilateral economic policy coordination.

Should efforts to overcome the current very serious constitutional crisis fail, no provincial government, including Ontario or Quebec, could conceivably claim the international strength and influence to justify the kind of representation that Canada now merits in international councils of all kinds. A re-configured Canada without Quebec, which cannot now be excluded, would be vastly diminished in economic, political/military, and moral terms, and an independent Quebec would count for even less. The Canadian foreign policy whole is, and will be, manifestly greater than the sum of its parts.

Even the "worst-case" outcomes of the Canadian constitutional crisis (however those might be defined) are unlikely to produce dangerous international destabilization, but one final link between the changing international environment and the resolution of Canada's constitutional crisis is frequently underestimated by Canadians. In a world where a growing challenge is the accommodation of ethnic, linguistic and regional diversity with the demands of interdependence and integration, Canada has to date been seen as one of the most successful role-models. The European Community itself, through acceptance of economic integration and common standards in vital areas such as human rights, is gradually moving to develop on a massive scale but short of the federal model, something like the kind of community that Canada has already evolved.

Any Canadian constitutional outcome that is seen internationally as a failure of the Canadian experiment in tolerance, accommodation and cooperation would damage confidence, in less-favored parts of the world, that open, democratic societies can manage these challenges. Together with the direct value placed on Canada's international representation and participation in confronting global challenges, this is an additional interest in the evolution of the Canadian state shared by Trilateral partners and others around the world.

III. JAPAN AND TRILATERAL COOPERATION

For the entire postwar period, Japan's foreign policy has been dominated by relations with the United States. The Japanese government made a conscious decision to base its external relations on this bilateral relationship, but it was also a matter of necessity arising out of Japan's defeat in the Pacific war. Over time, the relationship changed from one of occupier to ally and eventually to "equal partner." The United States was both a provider of security and by far Japan's most important economic partner. It also sponsored Japan's reacceptance into the international community. The United States, therefore, helped create a generally congenial international environment that enabled Japan to go without serious review of its own international position and role. But as Japan became a major economic power, the United States also become a principal source of demands that Japan equitably "share international responsibilities." These escalating pressures have bewildered the Japanese.

The Evolution of Trilateralism

It was with the encouragement of the United States that Japan began its initial exploration of Trilateralism some two decades ago. The Trilateral Commission itself was important in this process, having as a major objective the full participation of Japan as a member of the community of advanced, democratic nations. Another important step was the establishment of the Economic Summits in 1975, a grouping in which Japan, already the second largest market economy, naturally was included. The first oil shock had brought home to the Japanese as no other event the interdependence of the world economy. In the 1970s, however, only a very small minority of Japanese appreciated the interdependence of international security. Trilateralism was regarded basically as an economic concept and largely as an extension of the bilateral relationship with the United States.

Events at the end of the 1970s began to change Japanese perceptions, resulting in a growing acceptance within a small elite of a broader concept of Trilateralism. The Soviet intervention in Afghanistan gave credence to American claims that the Soviet Union was an expansionist power and demonstrated the commonality of North American, European, and Japanese interests in containing the Soviet security threat. Soviet deployments of intermediate-range SS-20 missiles in Europe as well as Asia further underscored the indivisibility of security in the two regions. At the 1983 Williamsburg Summit, Japan associated itself with a statement supporting Western arms control positions, thus establishing for the first time official Japanese recognition of Japan's stake in European security.

Japanese interest in Europe grew slowly, partly stimulated by concern over what appeared to be a decline in U.S. global capabilities in the late 1970s and partly by concerns about unilateralism in U.S. policy. Some Japanese argued that Japan and Western Europe needed to consult more closely and even coordinate their positions toward their common large ally. This line of thinking, however, did not proceed very far, both because of concern it might endanger the more important U.S. relationship and because Europe, more than the United States, seemed to regard Japan unidimensionally as an economic threat with little relevance to European security issues. To the Japanese, the European Community's goal of "completing the internal market" by the end of 1992 only seemed to accentuate the distance between Europe and Japan. Japanese feared that Europe would turn inward and increase its discrimination against Japan. This fear was one of the forces strengthening Japanese interest in Asia-Pacific economic cooperation including Canada and the United States.

Japan's Strategic Choices

At the beginning of the 1990s, Japan stands at a strategic crossroads. In one direction lies increasing global involvement as "a member of the West," that is, a full Trilateral partner. A second option is Asia-Pacific regionalism including North America but excluding Europe, as in the new APEC (Asia-Pacific Economic Cooperation) framework. Another possible route is to emphasize Japan's leadership in an Asian community above its Trilateral role, as in the East Asian Economic Group (EAEG) proposed in December 1990 by Prime Minister Mahathir of Malaysia. A fourth route is the one of political-security isolationism. More than any other single factor, the stresses in the U.S.-Japan relationship—sharply aggravated by the crisis in the Gulf and the December 1990 breakdown in the GATT Uruguay Round negotiations—have given rise to a mini-debate on these strategic options. The developments in the Soviet Union and Europe, both west and east, have also contributed to a rethinking of Japan's international role.

The Trilateral Option

The developments of the 1980s might have made the Trilateral option, buttressed by a secondary involvement in an Asia-Pacific community, the natural outcome for Japan's future foreign policy. Many factors, including the strong web of interdependent economic relationships and political interests among the advanced democracies, continue to make Trilateralism the preferred option among the Japanese foreign policy elite, although a form of Trilateralism still skewed strongly toward the United States rather than Europe.

The gradual acceptance of "Trilateralism" by the Japanese during the 1980s received a setback as the result of developments during 1990 in the Persian Gulf and the Uruguay Round, and showed the basic weaknesses of the Japanese commitment to an outward, internationalist foreign policy based on sharing global responsibilities. Japanese understanding of the need for Trilateral cooperation is still confined to small groups. These include the Foreign Ministry and other parts of the bureaucracy with an institutional commitment to internationalism, and a limited number of internationalized businessmen, politicians, and persons in academia and the media.

This narrow base means that advocates of sharing global responsibilities with Trilateral partners find it very difficult to win concrete support for their position when major sacrifices are involved. For example, Japan prides itself on a record of support for freer trade positions in the GATT, but on the critical and largely symbolic issue of concessions on opening the rice market, the ruling party proved unwilling and unable to make concessions to international trading partners. Similarly in the Gulf War, Japan gave rhetorical support for the position of most of the its Trilateral partners, but financial contributions came grudgingly at first and the government failed in an effort to create a peacekeeping corps to carry out civilian functions.

The Gulf crisis presented Japan with a major—and perhaps premature—test of Trilateralism, exposing the constraints that Japan has yet to overcome in participating fully in Trilateral cooperation. In particular, it starkly raised the question of whether Japan's preferred approach of bearing major international responsibilities without being a military power is indeed a viable one. In this instance, the Japanese government found that it could make only the most token of non-financial contributions in the face of a major threat to the interests of Japan and its Trilateral partners.

This Gulf crisis also came at a time of weak domestic political leadership, following a major political scandal from which the ruling party has not yet fully recovered. Despite the LDP's victory in the February 1990 lower house elections, there has been unusual political instability within the ruling party and this has made it unusually vulnerable to criticism from the opposition parties. This left the Japanese bureaucracy without the necessary political back-up for a position of more vigorous support for the international coalition confronting Iraq.

Other Options

Trilateralism may be regarded as the equivalent of global cooperation. Asia-Pacific regionalism is not necessarily inconsistent with Trilateralism any more than is European integration. In recent years, Japan has supported Asia-Pacific regionalism, including North American countries, as complementary to its Trilateral connections. The Asia-Pacific Economic Cooperation (APEC) process, for example, is viewed within the government as consistent with and adding to Japan's membership in institutions that link it with the Atlantic world such as the G-7 and the OECD. Trilateralism, it is pointed out, does not include countries of great importance to Japan including China, Korea, and the ASEAN group.

The United States is usually welcomed as a part of the Asia-Pacific community; in fact the Japanese government made it clear to the Australians that this was a precondition for Japanese participation when the APEC proposal was first bruited by Australian Prime Minister Hawke in early 1988 without including the United States or Canada. Should Trilateralism falter, Japan would not necessarily be uncomfortable with its primary identity in a broad Asia-Pacific grouping.

Some Japanese nationalists, however, favor placing a narrower Asian regionalism, excluding North America, above either Asia-Pacific regionalism or Trilateralism. Those who advocate this approach are dubious of the value to Japan of Trilateralism in which Japan, they believe, will always be dominated by other powers or isolated from real decision-making power in the alliance. On the other hand, they argue, Japan would be the leader of an Asian bloc.

This view, while emotionally attractive to some Japanese, in practice has many difficulties. While other Asian countries desire Japanese economic assistance, they are certain to resist a Japanese-dominated bloc. Ironically, it is, perhaps, only a Japan that is closely associated with the West that would be acceptable as a partner in Asia. Moreover, there is fear in Japan that a narrower Asian grouping would work to isolate Japan from its major trade and investment partner—the United States. For this reason, reaction in the Japanese government and business community to the Malaysian EAEG proposal has been cool at best. Although the Malaysian government has argued for the proposal as insurance against European and North American "economic blocs," the Japanese fear that an EAEG may encourage the very tendencies toward blocism in other regions that it is supposed to counteract.

Finally, in any Asian option, Japan must take into account its very large neighbor China. Although Japan is the economic giant of Asia, China has almost ten times its population and occupies a central geostrategic position. Should Japan seek to develop a primary international identity as the leader of an Asian grouping, it will be challenged by China, and the narrow context of Asian regionalism could encourage destabilizing Sino-Japanese competition. Such tendencies would be mitigated in a broader Asia-Pacific grouping developed as a complement to globalism.

The other option is political-security isolationism (economic isolationism is impossible). Japan would be responsible for its own security, and not seek an active multilateral role in shaping the post-Cold War world. In theory such a position could be compatible not only with unarmed neutrality, a position still formally advocated by the Japan Socialist Party, but also with a more assertive independent security and defense policy.

The quality of Japan's relations with the United States and Europe will be an important factor affecting Japan's choice of foreign policy options. Economic forces and values almost certainly push Japan in the direction of Trilateralism. But the emotional fear of being rejected by the West and forced to "change Japanese culture" can strengthen the forces of inward-looking Asian regionalism or isolationism.

Japan is in a dilemma, in that support for Trilateralism from its Western partners is both politically necessary and politically harmful. The need arises from the absence of a domestic political consensus supporting an internationalist foreign policy. Lacking the necessary leadership and will to make politically controversial adjustments, Japan has relied on foreign pressures (*gaiatsu*) to push forward both economic liberalization and a stronger political-security role. The recent Structural Impediments Initiative (SII) negotiations with the United States provide an example of this process; in this case foreign pressures were basically compatible with needs in the Japanese domestic economy, but change would not have occurred as early without these pressures.

The potential harm for Trilateralism arises from the clumsy and seemingly high-handed manner in which these pressures are often applied. The seeming failure of Japan's Trilateral partners to appreciate Japan's political difficulties and past concessions has resulted in an increasing political backlash against these pressures. The wide publicity given to Shintaro Ishihara's theme of "a Japan that can say 'no'" reflects the strains and backlash in Japanese domestic society. It also feeds further belief in the West that Japan does not fully appreciate Western contributions to Japan's security and economic environment and will share burdens only when confronted with tougher pressures. This vicious circle has been corrosive of the relationship with Japan's Trilateral partners and is potentially explosive. It also works to distort international issues, such as the Gulf crisis, into questions of U.S.-Japan relations and contributes to the impression that the other Trilateral partners are "ganging up" on Japan.

Overcoming this process of relying on foreign pressures, especially those from the United States, is vital to Japan's integration as a full Trilateral partner. To try to soften the chauvinistic emotionalism that has been associated with the U.S.-Japan relationship, it needs to be placed in a broader international framework. Trilateralism is such a framework.

Preparing Japan as a Trilateral Partner

The key challenge for Japan is to develop a new consensus on its international role. The old consensus, developed in the early postwar years and frequently dubbed the "Yoshida doctrine," was premised on the need for Japan to reconstruct its economy and abstain from an international politico-security role. Although Japan has adjusted its policies in line with growing international pressures, much of the prevailing thinking about foreign policy reflects the outdated premises of the Yoshida years. Japan needs to develop a foreign policy suitable to a major actor in an interdependent world. To be appropriately designed and implemented, this policy needs understanding and support beyond the narrow groups now advocating internationalism.

The lack of broad Japanese interest in foreign policy reflects the relatively favorable circumstances in which Japan found itself during most of the Cold War period. The combination of a strong bureaucracy, single-party rule, and a favorable international environment created a situation in which there was little apparent need for or interest in public policy debate on foreign policy or, for that matter, many domestic issues. The first priority for Japan's leaders must be to broaden political interest in foreign policy issues, thus providing a stronger base of support for Trilateralism.

There are four interrelated dimensions to this task:

First, Japan needs to reassess its international position and role. This requires that it come to terms with its history and the implications of that history for its international and particularly regional relations. Japan should reassess both its prewar and wartime experiences and its postwar growth as a major power. Japan needs to have a sound understanding of the constraints on its international role as well as the expectations placed upon it.

A second dimension is that of "internationalizing" Japanese attitudes and outlooks. This involves developing an understanding and acceptance of the values of others and a sense of world community. It also involves developing an appreciation that Japanese policies, in combination with those of its Trilateral partners, can have an impact on international events. In particular, Japan's domestic political leadership needs to be internationalized.

Third, adjustments are needed both in Japanese domestic policies and in the process by which those policies are determined. Particularly in the economic system, many policies and practices originated at the time the Japanese government led the effort to reconstruct and develop the Japanese economy. This led to a high degree of bureaucratic tutelage and protection and to the development of internal rules inconsistent with those being practiced elsewhere in the world.

Finally, appropriate changes in foreign policies can be made based upon the above transformations. These foreign policies should be rooted in independent Japanese analyses of the international environment and Japan's interests rather than cast in terms of accommodation of Western partners. However, given similar values and interests, it can be anticipated that Japanese foreign policies will be compatible and consistent with those of other Trilateral countries.

These tasks are ultimately the responsibility of the Japanese. Japan's Trilateral partners, however, are very important. Joint analysis of issues, consultations about common courses of action, and complementary policies to achieve shared goals play a central role in binding Japan to its Trilateral partners. The Trilateral Commission, and other institutions in which Europeans, North Americans, and Japanese work together in partnership, stimulate new thinking within Japan.

A key constraint for Japan lies in the field of human resources. Europe and North America have significant traditions of international involvement, which both legitimize their overseas roles and encourage the development of expertise—in both the public and private sectors—that can be brought to bear in complex overseas situations. Japan has a postwar foreign policy tradition of cultivating friendship in a relatively low-key manner and of advancing Japanese economic interests. As stressed above, in this environment there continues to be a tremendous need for an educational process of alerting the Japanese to their stake in international cooperation.

IV. A CHANGING EUROPE AND TRILATERAL COOPERATION

Among the three Trilateral partners, Europe has experienced the most dramatic changes during the almost two decades since the Trilateral Commission was formed. Developments from 1973, when Henry Kissinger proclaimed the "Year of Europe" to encourage and support developments toward European unity, through 1989, the "Anno Mirabilis" in which the division of Europe was overcome, have brought about fundamental changes. The Cold War has come to an end; the post-World War II bipolar order separating Western and Eastern Europe (and thus West and East Germany) has given way to opening borders. Poland, Hungary, and Czechoslovakia (CSFR) have overcome Communist rule and are developing democratic governments and institutions.

Independence movements within the Soviet Union have begun to threaten the cohesion, if not the very existence of this imperial empire. The Baltic States are close to national independence; Georgia, the homestate of Stalin, has declared its independence from the Union. The Warsaw Pact, once the Soviet Union's formidable instrument of political and military control of Eastern Europe and a permanent threat to Western Europe, has been dissolved. COMECON, its economic counterpart, has practically broken down. The Soviet Union is increasingly running what is left of its foreign trade on a U.S. dollar or German mark basis.

Within months after the Berlin Wall was torn down, Germany was on the road to reunification. Eleven months after the Wall was opened, Germany was reunited, allied control over Berlin was terminated, and full sovereignty returned to a reunited Germany within the borders defined after World War II.

Revolutionary, yet peaceful change has swept over Europe. It was channeled by the Helsinki process and stabilized by the European Community. Indeed, the Community of Twelve—developed from the Community of Six during the past two decades—has become and proved to be the only pole of stability in Europe. It has shown remarkable strength to absorb the shocks of change. Its own momentum, generated by the decision to complete the single internal market by 1993 and by its members' determination to establish a currency union and to push for political union, gave stability to the rapid process of change in Central Europe. The Community supported through its institutional framework the reunification of Germany and, by blending German unification with European integration, helped to overcome the anxieties a united Germany might otherwise have provoked among its neighbors in West and East. The European peace order established by the Community of the Twelve has given and continues to give guidance and encouragement to Central and Eastern European countries hoping to participate, thus broadening the base for a permanent order of peace in Europe.

Europe's Uncertain Identity

Revolutionary change, even if it successfully overcomes old dangers and threats, leads to new problems and uncertainties. In the Trilateral context, one of the more important uncertainties is that of Europe's identity. As our discussions and written contributions during the preparation of this report showed, the answer to the question "Who are we?" is far from certain.

The Institutional Development of the Community

Uncertainty begins with the future structure and institutional arrangements of the European Community itself. There is agreement that the process leading toward full economic union is irreversible. No one doubts that the single market among the Twelve will be completed by 1993. Political cohesion, if not union at the European Community level, is also seen as a top priority for the future of Europe. The deepening of the European Community, as opposed to its broadening to include new members, appears to many as one of the most important steps in building a new Europe and paving the way for successful integration of Central and Eastern Europe into this new entity. Only a more cohesive Community in economic, monetary and political terms is considered capable of controlling the risks built into present European and international developments. It is therefore considered vital for the European Community to strive for closer coordination in the foreign, security, and defense policy areas. The "European pillar" within the Atlantic defense system should be finally developed in such a way as to present a real equivalent to the American pillar.

Although there is no real disagreement on the need for political union in the European Community, there is still a wide range of opinions as to the intensity of political integration, the speed of the process, its relation to acceptance of new members (especially from among the EFTA states), and its consequences for democratic institutions of member-states as well as those to be developed for a European political union. Thus, while supporting the political union of Europe, some feel that, given the powers which will be accumulated by the institutions of the Community, there will have to be a considerable degree of genuine respect for decentralization and states' rights to correspond with the enormous size and diversity of the European Community. Others stress the need for an institutional framework for Europe that is fundamentally democratic in character. This means that the existing semi-democratic structures should be replaced by fully democratic bodies. Decisions on Community matters should be subject to democratic control. This implies the existence of an executive that is fully responsible to the European Parliament in the same manner as the executives of member-states are responsible to their parliaments.

Although fully democratic institutions are most desirable for a politically united Europe, it is unlikely that they can be established in the near future. Not only national governments, but also national parliaments may want to retain more control over the European process than would be compatible with full democracy on the European level. Thus a certain ambivalence as to the institutional development of the European Community will be most likely to continue to exist for some time to come.

Central and Eastern Europe

European identity will no doubt be influenced by the acceptance of new members into the Community and by future relations with the Central and Eastern European countries. There seems to be agreement now in the Community that EFTA states should be accepted as members, if and when they apply, provided they are willing to accept the full discipline of membership as it exists today and is about to develop through the decisions of the two inter-governmental conferences on currency union and political union. Jacques Delors' formula of "concentric circles" finds wide support among Community members. They agree that the first circle around the Community should be formed by the EFTA countries, the second by Central European countries (such as Poland, Hungary and the CSFR), and the third by the South-East European countries (Balkans) and the Soviet Union; and that membership in the Community or closer association should be granted in line with the sequence of these circles.

Even if enlargement in the near future is restricted to EFTA countries, their acceptance will raise problems as to the structure of decision-making, which even today, with twelve members, is quite complex. In particular, such enlargement would raise difficulties about the participation of representatives of each member-state in the Commission and in the Council of Ministers.

The Twelve therefore prefer to deepen the existing Community and complete the single internal market before new members are accepted. The Community, it is felt, needs time to complete its internal consolidation before accepting new members. New members at this stage would dilute the strength of the Community and jeopardize its objectives.

As to the second circle, no urgency to decide about membership exists, because none of these countries is ready for membership. Their economies are not sufficiently developed to be able to participate in the single market on a competitive basis, nor have their democratic institutions proven to be stable enough for immediate membership. Both economic and political development in these countries should be supported by the Community, and encouraged by the prospect of future membership or close association.

One factor that might influence the timetable for expanding Community institutions to the East and Southeast is a deepening rift between rich and poor countries in Europe. The resurgence of a new division of the European continent between rich and poor—now that the political, ideological and military divisions have been overcome—is indeed one of the major risks facing Europe in the years to come. The implications of such a new division are numerous and grave. One of them is the danger of East-to-West migration on a large scale.

Such migration will undoubtedly begin if Western Europe does not meet its special responsibility to help the Eastern European states to manage the critical period of transition from state-directed to market economies and to stabilize their new democratic political institutions. This assistance will have to include massive public aid as well as private investments. This assistance must encourage political development. Thus Western Europe should show a readiness to, if necessary, enforce certain political conditions linking aid to the process of reform. Such political conditions to benefit democratic governments in Eastern Europe are much more likely to be accepted from the European Community than from individual member-governments. The Europeanization of the assistance to Eastern European states is therefore a *sine qua non* for the success of any such program.

This special Western European responsibility may be called upon much sooner and on a much larger scale than originally anticipated. The economies in Central and Eastern Europe have practically broken down. The situation is even worse in the Soviet Union. Most of the Eastern European countries lack the managerial, administrative and cultural know-how that would enable them to operate liberal market economies. Their populations have been trained to subordinate themselves to the structures of a state-organized command economy. They have no experience with coordinated economic activities typical of market economies. They lack the skills of self-organization beyond the level of primitive barter and trade. These deficiencies cannot be overcome in short periods of time.

It is very doubtful that the entire populations of these countries will be willing to wait for significant improvements in their individual living conditions, to wait until their domestic economies can fully supply their needs and demands. Many will try to escape the burden of reconstruction of their devastated economies by moving west, thus jeopardizing the success of any reconstruction program that might be supported by the European Community.

To eliminate the migration threat at its roots might require a much larger effort (both financially and otherwise) than is presently discussed. The need for such a larger effort may in turn lead to tensions within the European Community, since some members are more directly affected by East-to-West migration than others. All this could slow down the process of currency and political union within the Community.

"Roman Europe" or Common European House?

The migration issue and, more generally speaking, the definition of Western European relations with the East will confront the European Community with a basic decision: whether to base its future identity on what could be called "Roman Europe" or to pursue the idea of a Common European House advanced most strongly by Mikhail Gorbachev, including the peoples of South-East Europe and the Soviet Union (that is, the third circle). Europe in this latter case would not only overcome its recent division, caused by the postwar bipolar order in Europe. It would set out to overcome its centuries-old division into a Roman and Byzantine Europe, and define itself in the way de Gaulle used to: from the Atlantic to the Urals.

There is no certainty as to which of the two concepts of Europe Europeans in the end will prefer. The consequences of each of the two concepts are markedly different. Should Europe continue with the time-honored partition into a Roman and Byzantine Europe, the Europe we are concerned with in the Trilateral partnership would end at the eastern border of Poland. Poland could eventually be accepted as a member; the same would be true for Hungary, the CSFR, and possibly Slovenia and Croatia, if both should separate from Yugoslavia. Migration within this Europe would be considered European migration and treated in the same fashion as migration was treated within the European Community in the 1960s. Migration from other Eastern European countries would not be permitted beyond possible quotas established by the European Community. Neither the Soviet Union nor its peoples would be admitted as members of an enlarged European Community, security systems such as the Helsinki process notwithstanding. Europe would not include the third of the three concentric circles defined by President Delors.

Europe's Trilateral partners will most likely suggest that Europe opt for the "Roman Europe," thus defining its identity along "Western" lines. They can point to the fact that "Byzantine Europe" is separated from the West by deep cultural and historical differences. The age of enlightenment, which has shaped Western European, North American and to a considerable degree also Japanese culture and civilization has had little influence on the development of most of the Soviet Union. No one doubts that it will take more than a generation to bring about the political, economic and cultural developments that are the prerequisite for liberal market economies and truly democratic governments. The political, economic and cultural maturity which is the result of hundreds of years of evolutionary development in Western Europe and the Western world can hardly be acquired in the short period of one or two generations.

To opt for the Western definition of Europe would also be in line with the evolution of the European Community during the past 40 years. There can be no doubt that the idea of European union, which dates back to European movements after the First World War, was originally intended to overcome the historic enmity between France and Germany and to bring about a European political order that would provide means for a peaceful settlement of European conflicts. The successful implementation of this idea based on Monnet's concept of a Coal and Steel Community and put into institutional form by Adenauer, de Gaulle and de Gasperi was greatly helped by the need for Western Europe and North America to defend themselves against the Soviet threat. The European Community was strongly influenced both in its development and in its perception by the bipolar Cold War order in Europe. It did constitute the major part of "Roman Europe" even as East Germany, Poland, Hungary and the CSFR were under Soviet domination. Never did the European Community view itself as the trustee of Eastern Europe or the peoples of the Soviet Union. For decades the Community was a Western community. European integration was West European integration.

It is therefore not surprising that the Declaration on EC-U.S. Relations of November 23, 1990, which establishes an institutional framework for consultation, implicitly defines Europe as Western Europe. As a common goal of the European Community and the United States, it states the determination of both parties and the EC member-states to strengthen their partnership in order to "provide adequate support...to the nations of Eastern and Central Europe undertaking economic and political reforms and encourage their participation in the multilateral institutions of international trade and finance." This objective of cooperation is listed together with the resolve of the parties to the Declaration "to help developing countries by all appropriate means in their efforts toward political and economic reform." There is no language in the Declaration indicating that the parties intend Eastern and Central Europe to become part of the European Community and thus create a Common European House such as might result from the Helsinki process.

It is impossible to determine at this time which of the two alternatives Europeans may finally chose. Many indications make it seem likely that Western Europe will continue to be the basis for European identity. As a result, our Trilateral partners, although aware of an expansion of the European Community to include the EFTA countries and the "second circle" countries of Central Europe, can continue to count on a Western-oriented Europe sharing the order of values that has so deeply influenced the development of all Trilateral partners. On the other hand, Europe's responsibility for the developments in Eastern Europe will be a special one that cannot be compared with its responsibility for the developing world. Not only our security and the problem of migration, but also the need to meet an existential ecological challenge to all of geographic Europe, make it imperative to get involved in Eastern European developments. Thus basic interests of West Europeans might commit an expanding European Community to devote substantial economic, financial and political resources in support of East European reconstruction and, by doing so, to assume political responsibilities that go far beyond normal aid to developing countries.

German Unification

In the course of the liquidation of the division of Europe, Europeans and our Trilateral partners were especially concerned about the possible consequences of German unification. Although unification was welcomed and supported by the United States and Canada, Japan, and the other members of the EC, questions were raised as to the possible consequences for the European process in general and future German contributions in particular. Many were concerned that Germany, under the burden of reconstructing the eastern part of the country, might divert more resources into the process of unification than would be compatible with European integration and responsibility. Others saw the possibility of an inward-looking Germany, fully involved in the process of unification, reconstruction and redefinition of its national and European identity.

Future developments will show most of these concerns to be unwarranted. To begin with, the economic burden of rebuilding the depleted capital stock in the eastern part of Germany and of revitalizing the former GDR's economy is not as large as assumed by many. Although substantial in absolute terms, the necessary transfer from West to East Germany amounts to only about 3-4 percent of GNP—in other words, to the growth of GNP in one or two years. The burden on the West German population therefore does not exceed that of two years without real growth of GNP. Once established as a continuing transfer to support reconstruction in the East until it is completed, these financial payments will not be felt as a politically or economically harmful limitation on the economic development of West Germany. As growth in the eastern parts gains momentum— most likely in 1993—and as the completion of the Community's single market produces additional growth opportunities, most of the economic and political cost of German unification will be absorbed, when viewed in terms of long-range political and economic strategy.

As to continued support for European union, Germany has always treated the process of unity as a European rather than a strictly German matter. It was clear from the outset that German unity could only be won in the process of creating European unity. Germans remain fully aware of the fact that without revolutionary change in Poland, in Hungary, and in the CSFR, German unification would not have been possible. Germans more than other European peoples have learned to understand that not the nation-state, but a blend of European political union and regional autonomy within federal states is the political structure most compatible with the political, cultural, economic and ethnic diversity of Europe. They have therefore always supported decentralization of power in Europe, regional self-government, and a serious application of the principle of subsidiarity.

It is true that Germany has, and will have for some time, difficulties in finding and defining its new identity as a united country. The cultural and psychological differences that developed during 40 years of separation into two antagonistic ways of life have left deep marks that cannot be overcome quickly. However, even in this context the European dimension of the process will help further to assure Germans that there is no alternative to a European Germany. German preoccupation with unification will therefore not stand in the way of European development.

European-American Relations

There is no doubt among Europeans that U.S.-European relations will continue to be of major importance for the development and the security of Europe. However, with the end of the Cold War and its bipolar order of confrontation, the nature of this relationship has changed. During the Cold War the United States was the undisputed "leadership nation" of the West. NATO was the most important framework for cooperation. Disputes and conflicts between the Atlantic partners were not permitted to obscure the overriding importance of the common security and defense efforts of Western Europe and North America.

The United States supported the movement towards European unity. It wanted Europe to unite, develop a defense posture of its own, and become one of the "pillars" on which the Atlantic Alliance was based. Although NATO was not restricted to common defense, but was to serve as an overall alliance based on common values and facilitating broad political and economic cooperation, common defense was clearly the main objective of NATO and the United States its leading power.

Now that the major threats of the Cold War have been eliminated and Europe is in the process of developing an all-European identity, NATO's role has changed from a dominant one to one complementary to other institutional arrangements serving European security and unity. For the development of a system of European peace, many Europeans look more to the development of the Helsinki process and/or the political structures of a politically united Europe. Even though the development of such a peace order may take time and not materialize within the next ten to fifteen years, nothing should be done that could get in the way of such a European security system based on the idea of a Common European House.[1]

These developments require a substantial adjustment on the part of the United States. Nothing less than a change from "leadership nation" to "partnership nation" is called for. It is not surprising that such a process of adjustment and change causes friction and irritation. Hence the complaints by the United States about European tendencies to resolve internal European problems without adequate consultation with the United States, or the general feeling that U.S. interests are being "pushed to the back burner." Europeans do not want the United States to become in effect a thirteenth member of the European Community. The United States does not want to be separated from the European process now that its protective shield is no longer required with the same degree of urgency.

What seems to amount to an alienation between the two sides of the Atlantic within the Trilateral partnership is in reality the expression of the process of adjustment to the revolutionary change in European conditions. The adjustment, however, takes place in a framework of broad consensus on basic values, of a common heritage, and of common beliefs in the purposes and objectives of human society. This framework is much stronger and much more stable than recent concerns voiced by Americans and Europeans alike might lead us to believe. What is called for, as in earlier periods of tension and irritation, is a broad dialogue between the United States and Europe. It could serve to explain to the United States the significance of changes in Europe, the nature and scope of the new European challenge, and the strength and possibilities that may result from the European process. To Europeans it might explain the special U.S. problem of redefining its role as leading nation in the world, as well as its efforts to cope with domestic and Western Hemisphere problems that may not be familiar to Europeans.

Provisions for such a dialogue have been made by the EC-U.S. Declaration of November 1990 mentioned above. But the dialogue cannot be left to governments and official contacts. It must be

---

[1] As to European responsibilities outside the NATO area, most Europeans agree that NATO is not the appropriate instrument with which to meet such responsibilities. They should rather be met in the framework of the United Nations.

broadened to include industry, the labor unions, the academic community, and the media. Given the long-standing relationship between the United States and Europe, the present lack of knowledge on each side about the other is surprisingly distinct. In the 1950s and 1960s, thousands of exchanges—Europeans to U.S. universities, the great number of European immigrants in the United States, and American elites who had received part of their education in Europe—helped to maintain a broad dialogue between Europe and the United States. Present-day leaders on each side of the Atlantic do not command the same kind of knowledge about developments on the other side. It is this deficit more than a lack of institutional arrangements that could contribute to an estrangement between the United States and Europe as a consequence of rapid change. The Trilateral partnership has an important role in preventing such a development by encouraging cooperation and dialogue on all levels of society.

European-Japanese Relations

European-Japanese relations are the least developed among two Trilateral partners. They mainly center around issues of trade (e.g., opening of markets, possible discrimination) and common responsibilities that result from the large world roles of the Japanese and European economies. The bipolar world dividing Europe and concentrating its efforts on security and defense within the framework of NATO may have stood in the way of developing closer political relations with Japan and of identifying common global responsibilities of both Europe and Japan. In this case, the end of the Cold War could open new areas of common interests. One such area could be participation in the development of the Soviet economy, especially its Asian parts.

Aside from the challenges posed by the Soviet Union to both Japan and Europe, there are numerous new tasks that can be successfully undertaken only if the three Trilateral partners, as the leading economies of the world, work together. Among these, the consequences of overpopulation of our planet and of the progressive destruction of its ecological base are the most urgent. Regardless of possible institutional arrangements that may emerge in the framework of the United Nations, close cooperation among Japan, Europe and North America is imperative if we are to secure a safe world in the 21st Century.

V. A Reshaped Trilateral Agenda

One of the problems of cooperation in the post-Cold War period will be finding ways to dramatize the benefits of cooperation, to represent the long-run self-interest of countries, and to escape from the veto power of particular groups. The decline of Soviet power and the diminished appeal of Communist ideology have removed the overarching threat that was dramatically clear to public opinion in the Trilateral democracies. Powerful economic groups in modern democracies often have veto powers which can thwart the growth of economic interdependence, even when it is beneficial for society as a whole. The task of cooperation will be doubly difficult because, as discussed above, each of the three major areas of the Trilateral world will be increasingly preoccupied with its own internal affairs.

Europe in particular will be enormously self-absorbed. The Federal Republic of Germany faces the task of economically and politically integrating the former eastern region into its democratic fabric. By some estimates, this may take the rest of the decade and a trillion dollars to implement fully. At the same time, the European Community will be preoccupied with perfecting the union among its twelve current members, as well as strengthening relations with its Scandinavian, neutral, and Eastern European neighbors.

In North America, Canada faces unprecedented centrifugal forces at home. At the same time, voices are heard in the United States casting doubt on the wisdom of continuing to bear such a large part of the burden of global leadership. Historically, Americans have oscillated between inward and outward orientations, and with the end of the Cold War threat, there are many Americans who feel that it is time to turn attention inward. Certainly, the agenda of domestic issues described above must be addressed. It remains possible for the United States to do this without turning its back on the rest of the world, but many in the domestic political debate cast the issue in terms of a simple dichotomy between domestic and foreign orientations.

Finally, Japan is still uncertain about its international role. Comfortable at home and fearing rejection abroad, many in Japan are reluctant to accept new international responsibilities, and many special interests take advantage of that political climate to persuade politicians to protect them from international competition.

These domestic trends in the three regions can lead to policies which reinforce each other at the cost of Trilateral cooperation. In such a setting, groups favoring cooperation will need to reinforce each other by forming coalitions across international borders. Among such groups would be the Trilateral Commission. The Commission can help the Trilateral countries to define their long-term common objectives. Despite common values, the three regions have somewhat different forms of democratic capitalism. Explaining and understanding cultural variations can be as important a task as coordinating policies in pursuit of common values. There will be no lack of challenges in the 1990s that will require Trilateral cooperation, but in the absence of an overarching threat such as characterized the Cold War years, the task of explaining the new challenges to our fellow citizens will be even more critical to an effective response than in the past. In the following pages we suggest a ten-point agenda—broad but not comprehensive—on which to concentrate Trilateral efforts.

THE CHALLENGES OF THE 1990s

1. Sustainable Global Economic Growth and Development

The Trilateral countries represent 60 percent of the world's product but only 12 percent of the world's population. More rapid population growth in the poorer parts of the globe will cause the Trilateral countries to become even more of a minority over time. China and India each already have larger populations than the Trilateral partners together. While ecological concerns are growing and resource management is increasingly important, there is no alternative to sustainable growth. The only long-run solution to the population problem is the demographic transition which occurs when higher standards of living are achieved. Economic development is a large part of the social change that persuades parents to have fewer children. The rich countries cannot expect stability if economic growth is halted. Economic conflicts and protectionism will hurt not only the rich countries, but also the poor.

Cooperation from developing countries will be needed to manage many of the growing problems of economic and ecological interdependence. The Trilateral countries need to promote successful development in poorer countries—more than increases in the standard of living for the privileged—in order to build a foundation for the commitment of these countries to the shared system. Through development assistance and institutions like the World Bank, it is important that the Trilateral countries follow policies which insure that growth spreads to other parts of the globe while attending to the quality of the environment. This will require technological developments which increase the efficient use of global resources. Improved energy efficiency, particularly in the United States, will be important. Above all, the wealthy countries must maintain an open international system which allows other countries to advance. This means the Trilateral countries must keep their own markets open and maintain a degree of monetary stability that encourages international trade and investment.

Detailed recommendations for environmental management or for monetary stability are beyond the scope of this report, but the Trilateral countries, as the largest players in the world economy, should see themselves as trustees of the public good of sustainable economic growth.[1] As trustees, they need to resist domestic veto groups, keep their markets open, and promote sustainable growth in the poorer parts of the world. The alternative, if they succumb to short-run pressures, is a deterioration in world conditions which would eventually come back to hurt the electorates in the Trilateral democracies.

2. Peaceful Change in the Declining Soviet Empire
The changes in the Soviet Union in the past decade have been among the most important causes of the transformation of world politics. There are two aspects to these changes: one is the failure of the centralized Stalinist economic system and the other is the new policies which allowed liberalization at home and abroad. The root cause of the Soviet decline is the inability of the centralized economic planning system to come to terms with the information-age economy. This failure became visible in the slowdown of Soviet economic growth in the 1970s and its stagnation in the 1980s. Returning to repression and renewed centralization will not reverse the decline of Soviet economic strength. On the contrary, since centralization was the root cause of decline, recentralization will accelerate it.

---

[1] Detailed recommendations regarding sustainable development are presented in another report to the Trilateral Commission published in 1991. See Jim MacNeill, Pieter Winsemius, and Taizo Yakushiji, *Beyond Interdependence: The Meshing of the World's Economy and the Earth's Ecology* (New York: Oxford University Press, 1991). On international monetary and financial stability, see Shijuro Ogata, Richard N. Cooper, and Horst Schulmann, *International Financial Integration: The Policy Challenges* (New York: The Trilateral Commission, 1989).

Nonetheless, a return to more repressive policies internally and increased use of the military may lead to a reversal of some of the "new thinking" in foreign policy. Here another distinction becomes important, that between the "inner empire" and the "outer empire." The "outer empire" in Eastern Europe disintegrated in 1989. While it is not impossible that the Soviets might attempt to reverse that change, it would be extremely costly. Without Soviet control of Eastern Europe and an effective Warsaw Pact, the threat of a short-warning attack against Western Europe loses credibility. So some changes in recent years are in effect irreversible.

As for the "inner empire," the multiethnic Soviet Union itself, the Trilateral countries do not have an interest in maintaining the exact borders of today's Soviet Union. They do, however, have an interest that any changes occur peacefully. Not only is there a concern for the disposition of Soviet nuclear weapons, but violence inside the Soviet Union could spill over its borders or produce flows of refugees which would put enormous strain on the social systems of neighboring countries. Moreover, the Trilateral countries have an interest in encouraging the development of political pluralization and a market economy in the Soviet Union. A more open and democratic Soviet Union (or Russia) will present less of a threat.

In policy terms, the internal contradictions of the Soviet system present hard choices. Our view is that providing major structural assistance and incorporating the Soviet Union into international economic institutions should be conditioned upon internal liberalization of the Soviet economy and political system. There are two reasons for this view. One is that it does no good to provide structural aid to the Soviet Union unless there are serious economic reforms. If there is a hole in a bucket, you don't pour water in it until the bucket is patched. The other reason for conditioning structural economic aid on liberalization is to provide incentives for reform and disincentives for the type of violent repression which was seen earlier this year in the Baltic Republics. Public opinion in the Western democracies will demand some response to violent repression and violation of human rights inside the Soviet Union. Given the continuing nature of our common interest with the Soviet Union in managing nuclear weapons, it would be a mistake to link arms control to Soviet domestic policies, but entirely appropriate to link economic aid.

We also distinguish emergency aid designed to stem chaos and disorder in the short run (and technical assistance and private transnational contacts to help foster reform) from major structural aid aimed at longer-run reform of the Soviet economy. We would be more flexible with emergency aid than with structural aid. The Trilateral countries will need to coordinate their positions on any major structural assistance. It would do no good if one country turned off the tap while another turned it on. Consultations which lead to a common understanding of the internal situation in the Soviet Union—the prospects for change and the effectiveness of various economic measures—will be important in formulating a common approach as the fate of the Soviet Union unfolds in the 1990s.

3. Successful Transition in Eastern Europe

The re-emergence of Eastern Europe in 1989 from more than four decades of Soviet control marked the end of the Cold War. Many in the West point to the peaceful revolutions in Eastern Europe as a triumph of liberal democratic values and human rights. Certainly the changes in 1989 greatly enhance the security of the Western countries. It would be tragic if the Trilateral countries fail to actively assist the transition to market economies, including access to Trilateral markets. If Eastern European countries slip back into autocracy of the left or right, the claims of a victory for liberal democracy will have a hollow ring and the security situation in Europe will worsen. If Eastern Europe degenerates into a set of weak and feuding states, the neighboring powers would probably be drawn in to provide order. Some see the collapse of weak regimes then leading Europe dangerously "back to the future."

The economic transition may be slow. While private investment will solve some of the problems of the region, it is important for Western governments to provide debt relief and bilateral assistance as well as support for the new Bank for European Reconstruction and Development. The cost of assisting market liberalization in the former Communist countries of Eastern Europe is far less than the cost of military containment, but our governments have not paid adequate attention to this comparison. Because change will take time, it is important for the European Community to hold out the prospect of future membership (and more immediate association) in the Community as a symbol of hope. Just as the European Community served as a magnet that encouraged democracy in Spain, Portugal, and Greece in the 1970s, so also it can draw the states of Eastern Europe toward liberal democratic values in the decade to come. While liberalization may be a slow process, it is important that the European Community promise that those who successfully move toward democratic politics and market economies will eventually be taken in. The Community will need to structure itself so that its membership can expand without making its internal procedures too cumbersome.

4. Further Integration of the European Community

The uniting of Europe in the framework of the Community has been a major contribution to the peace and prosperity of the world over the last half century. Europe's Trilateral partners have an interest that the process continues. The benefits of European integration depend very much on a European Community that remains open politically and economically to the rest of the world. There is always a danger that local preoccupations can divert European attention away from wider concerns and that problems internal to the Community may be solved at the expense of outsiders. On the other hand, what happens in Europe depends in part on those same outsiders. If Europe's Trilateral partners treat Europe as an entity, they can encourage the integration process; if they play off Europeans against one another and weaken the Brussels institutions, they can slow down the process. It is critical for the success of European integration that both sides keep the long-run common interest in sight.

Successful management of economic conflicts often depends upon an early warning system and on a web of informal and formal contacts across borders. In the past, security consultations in the context of NATO provided a rich web of contacts which helped to manage or to head off disputes between North America and Western Europe before they became intractable. With the prospect of a diminished role for NATO and increasing attention to the role of the European Community, early warning is more difficult to implement. Secretary of State James Baker called attention to this issue in a speech in Berlin in December 1989. The November 1990 "Transatlantic Declaration" was an important step in the direction of an answer. It provides for increased consultations between the Community and the United States at several levels. At the highest level, the President of the European Council and President of the European Commission will undertake consultations with the U.S. President twice a year. Similar arrangements have been put in place with Canada and are being worked out between European Community institutions and Tokyo. Even though such steps are useful, they may not be sufficient. It is important to continue developing informal contacts and procedures and to cease worrying about slogans like "informal vetoes" or "thirteenth seat at the table."

Greater interchange among parliamentarians can contribute to this process of better informal understanding.

Given the uncertainty of the outcome of the second Russian Revolution and the prospect of instability in Eastern Europe, a continued North American military presence in Europe provides a useful insurance policy. The demise of the Warsaw Pact, removing the danger of a short-warning attack, makes it possible to reduce the number of American troops from the high level of the Cold War years. Nevertheless, the existence of some American and Canadian forces on the Continent to couple European security to that of North America will still play a useful role. While Europe may gradually develop a greater capacity in foreign and defense policy, there will still be a role for NATO, and it would be a mistake to let NATO institutions atrophy. Someday NATO may work itself out of a job, but that is unlikely in the uncertain climate of the 1990s. Moreover, the cooperation that has developed among NATO states for the defense of the NATO area has proven useful for these states when, in their individual capacities, they have wanted to coordinate positions in "out-of-area" crises such as that in the Persian Gulf. Thus it would be a mistake to worry too much about the details of the architecture of European security while conditions are as turbulent as they are likely to be in the 1990s. Navigation and a sense of direction will be more important than the details of architecture. We should head in the direction of a greater European capacity to contribute to its own defense without removing the residual insurance policy provided by the American security guarantee.

Such a vision of the future also helps to remove concern about the potential conflict between NATO and the Conference on Security and Cooperation in Europe (CSCE). The two organizations fill quite different functions. CSCE helps to build confidence and provide points of contact for greater transparency and communication within the broader European security arena, but it does not replace the need for an insurance policy of the sort that NATO provides for the democracies of Western Europe.

5. Wider Global Roles for Japan

Involving Japan in more global roles through international institutions will be a major challenge for the 1990s. Japan's impressive growth has made it a potential disruptive force in the international economy as well as in international politics. Japan is now simply too large to be a free rider. A Japan that continued to export without attention to its effects on the international trading system could easily lead to the breakdown of the GATT system. Similarly, a Japan that reacted to the protectionist pressures of its partners with a militaristic regional approach to its economic and security problems could be a very destabilizing factor in the balance of power in East Asia. How Japan reacts to its new size and importance in international affairs will depend in part on its Trilateral partners. As Japan searches for a global role, its partners can make a large difference in how that role will be defined.

Too often both Japan and its partners have been content to see Japan simply as a banker, but financial contributions alone do not provide a sufficient global role for Japan. On the other hand, for historical reasons relating to stability in the East Asian region, it is important that Japan not try to provide for its own military security by becoming a military superpower. For this reason, Japan's contribution to peace in the East Asian region should be complemented by continuing the U.S. presence in Asia, including maintenance of the U.S.-Japan Security Treaty.

There are many steps possible within Japan's Constitution which go beyond financial assistance. For example, Japan should be encouraged to play a larger role in international institutions. Japan can do more to provide peacekeepers for United Nations operations; Japan can develop an international rescue corps; Japan can take a lead in providing more personnel and resources for important international institutions. Similarly, a Japanese lead on coordination of official development assistance and measures to improve the international ecology would be fruitful steps. Japanese provision of leadership for international institutions is to be welcomed and encouraged. The appointment of a distinguished Japanese woman as the United Nations High Commissioner for Refugees is an important step in the right direction. Perhaps it is time for a Japanese president of the one of the major international economic institutions. Similarly, in response to the uncertainties about the Soviet future, it is useful to have Japanese participation in institutions such as the CSCE. If security problems stretch from San Francisco to Vladivostok, Japan's role can no longer be seen only in the local East Asian context.

If Japan is to "say as well as pay," problems arise relating to Japan's role in the United Nations. Japan is the second largest economy in the world and the second largest contributor to the organization's budget, but it lacks a permanent seat on the Security Council. Someday in the distant future, one could imagine a Europe unified enough to accept the idea that the French and U.K. seats in the Security Council be merged into a single European seat, and the other seat given to Japan. There are no signs, however, of that happening in the near future. Moreover, any efforts to amend the Charter of the United Nations to provide a place for Japan would open Pandora's box. So many demands might arise for greater participation that the Security Council, which now has a promise of working more effectively in the post-Cold War era, might be reduced to immobility. One way to alleviate if not totally solve this problem would be to develop informal mechanisms. For example, Japan (and perhaps Germany) could be regularly re-elected to the Security Council. The permanent members of the Security Council discuss the agenda and their positions before each Security Council meeting. The permanent five could enlarge their informal circle to six (or seven), incorporating Japan in these meetings before the formal sessions of the Security Council. Since Japan will be asked to play a larger role both financially and in the provision of civilian peacekeepers for UN operations, such a presence is entirely appropriate.

6. United Nations Collective Security and Peacekeeping

For the 40 years of the Cold War, the collective security provisions of the United Nations Charter were largely in abeyance although the organization was often able to play useful if more modest peacekeeping roles. The response to Iraq's invasion of Kuwait was remarkable insofar as it was the first instance of the Security Council authorizing military action under Article 42 of the Charter since the Korean War in 1950. Had the Security Council failed in such a clear-cut case of aggression, collective security would have been a dead letter in the post-Cold War world order.

Nonetheless, it is important to acknowledge the limitations of the Persian Gulf case. The United Nations has always been more successful when borders are clearly crossed than in civil wars. Saddam Hussein's proclaimed annexation of Kuwait was a clear challenge to collective security. In the more murky circumstances of domestic conflict and civil war, there is a greater chance that one of the permanent members will veto Security Council action. It is also worth noting that when the Gulf crisis went beyond sanctions to military operations, there was a preponderant United States role. One of the questions for the future is whether it will be possible to develop a greater military role for the United Nations. When will it be appropriate to use such a force? This is a topic in which the Trilateral countries have an interest, but much deeper study is necessary. It might be a subject for a further Trilateral report.

What should happen if a veto prevents United Nations collective security or peacekeeping operations from being implemented in future regional crises? It is unlikely and unsuitable that the Trilateral countries should try to become policemen of a world legal order in circumstances where the United Nations is unable to cope. On the other hand, UN member-states retain a right to individual and collective self-defense under Article 51 of the UN Charter. It is appropriate for the Trilateral countries to have a political consultation mechanism where they can discuss the extent to which their interests are threatened and the extent to which informal cooperation can improve the prospects either for a UN role or for action on a more limited basis.

7. Non-Proliferation of Advanced Weapons Technology

Technology spreads with time, but restraints on exports can slow the rate of proliferation and buy time to establish more favorable political conditions. For example, in 1963 President John F. Kennedy expected that there would be 25 countries with nuclear weapons by the 1970s. In fact, there were probably nine by 1990. Various measures such as the Non-Proliferation Treaty and the Nuclear Suppliers Group guidelines have helped to slow the spread well below what was expected. With a slower rate of spread, there are more chances to manage the destabilizing effects. The aftermath of the Gulf War provides an opportunity to reinvigorate and expand various measures for restraint on the export of technologies related to advanced weaponry.

In the nuclear area, it is worth noting that the Non-Proliferation Treaty must be renewed by a majority vote of its member-states in 1995. Recent acceptance of the NPT by France is an encouraging development. In the area of ballistic missiles, the existing Missile Technology Control Regime includes seven countries from the Trilateral regions, but needs to be expanded to include such important suppliers as the Soviet Union and China. In regard to chemical weaponry, the best hope is completion of the chemical weapons convention currently being negotiated in Geneva. But controlling weapons of mass destruction is not enough. In the past, supplier nations have not been successful in implementing regimes for restricting the export of conventional weapons or dual-use technologies essential for advanced conventional weapons systems. A complete ban on the sale of conventional weaponry is not likely but it may be possible to organize supplier constraints on sales of weaponry to areas of tension, defined as regions or pairs of countries which have recently experienced (or seem about to experience) war or civil war.

It is impossible to ban all arms transfers because at the low-technology end of the spectrum there are more than two dozen suppliers. But at the high-technology end of the spectrum, the number of suppliers is small and includes primarily Trilateral countries. An effective agreement might be achieved, for example, in technologies related to jet engines, advanced sensors, and precision-guided weapons. It is worth noting the experience of COCOM during the Cold War, where members agreed upon specific systems or technologies which should not be sold. Exceptions were sometimes made, but the exceptions required discussion and agreement before they were granted. Such consultation helped to stiffen national export controls, and dampened destructive competition resulting in lowest-common-denominator outcomes. A high priority for the Trilateral countries in the 1990s will be organizing restraints on transfers of arms to areas of tension as well as strengthening existing regimes governing technologies related to weapons of mass destruction.

8. Means to Address Transnational Global Issues

Some of the new international challenges in the 1990s are deeply rooted in societies and not simply the consequences of governmental actions. Issues such as ecological dangers, migration, terrorism, and the transnational drug trade are examples of the diffusion of power to private, non-state actors in international affairs. Whereas the Soviet threat over the last four decades was clear-cut, the diffusion of power in the 1990s also involves a diffusion in the perception of danger. On many of these transnational issues, "the enemy is us." The nature of many of these new transnational issues and the types of institutions and cooperation needed to deal with them are not yet clear. Increasingly such issues do not simply place one state against another. Rather they are issues in which all states try to control non-state transnational actors or other private actors within their own (and each other's) societies.

Although military force may sometimes play a role, traditional instruments of power are rarely sufficient to deal with the new transnational issues. In some instances, such as ecological threats, it may be important to organize international agreements by which states will change domestic policies—concerning use of chlorofluorocarbons (CFCs), for example. In the area of drugs, sharing information about drug traffic and how to deal with reducing domestic demand—or working together to confront countries which are sources of drugs—may be more important. Similarly, in questions relating to terrorism, the sharing of information can be important, as well as efforts to isolate countries which provide havens. With regard to migration, the long-run economic effects of migration are often positive, but if the rate is too fast, migration can have disruptive political and cultural effects. In such circumstances, assistance in dealing with refugees and exchange of information and experience about coping with migration flows can help the Trilateral countries to deal with the issue.

9. More Attention to International Institutions

Governments are losing some of their ability to control private actors who easily cross national borders. Unilateral efforts to curtail interdependence often prove costly and ineffective. Thus the new challenges of the 1990s will require more attention to international institutions which coordinate action among governments. Some existing institutions are quite effective. In other cases, the Trilateral countries will need to develop new institutions or informal procedures to coordinate more effective action.

Multilateral institutions help governments in four major ways. They facilitate burden-sharing by establishing standards and procedures for consultation. They provide the shared information essential for effective action on issues that cross national borders. They facilitate diplomacy by giving government officials access to each other's policy-making process through negotiations and personal contacts which, in turn, allow them to anticipate more confidently their partners' reactions to hypothetical events. Finally, they establish rules and procedures which help to reinforce continuity and a long-term focus in contrast to what typically prevails in domestic politics. By representing long-term self-interest, institutions help to provide discipline in the politics of democracies. Institutions help to anchor transnational coalitions and focus larger interests.

For example, during the last half century, the world economy has benefited from international trade that has grown more rapidly than production. Part of the credit belongs to technological changes, but part also belongs to the GATT system which created a transnational coalition in favor of freer trade. Within each democracy, domestic interests that feel threatened by competition sue for governmental protection from outside influences, but the institutionalized promise of reciprocity in accepting exports of other nations created a countervailing transnational coalition in the domestic politics of the Trilateral countries. If the GATT system did not exist, or were allowed to deteriorate, all countries would be worse off.

Many of the new challenges to the Trilateral countries require domestic concerns to be discussed in an international context. Progress will involve more than governments. Informal institutional contacts and transnational coalitions will be increasingly important.

The Structural Impediments Initiative (SII) talks between the United States and Japan provide an interesting case in point. Contrary to initial concerns that discussion of domestic matters would prove intractable and only generate nationalist passions, the SII talks proved to be a modest success. Japanese consumers have not only profited from American pressure for improvements in the Japanese distribution system, but polls show that the Japanese public welcomed such actions. Similarly, American Congressmen and Administration officials who wished to address the problem of the budget deficit could point to commitments in the SII talks. As described in the chapter on Japan, one of the reasons the Structural Impediments Initiative was successful was that it was reciprocal. The other reason was that each side was pushing on a partly open door, i.e., urging the accomplishment of objectives that each of the governments had already conceded in principle were worthwhile but was finding difficult to implement because of domestic political divisions.

As the prominence of domestic concerns in Trilateral relations rises, we might think in terms of a "Trilateral SII." Governments must learn to accept the right of others to question how they act and establish procedures for probing each other's actions. By forming mutual pressure groups of this sort, the Trilateral countries can help to legitimize and multilateralize what the Japanese call *gaiatsu* or foreign pressure. By legitimizing and multilateralizing the mutual pressure, countries can reduce the degree of nationalistic reaction that is sometimes generated by such processes. In short, effective Trilateralism in the 1990s will require innovative ways to relate a more diffuse set of challenges to domestic politics in the democracies. Such procedures will involve both governmental and non-governmental action. For example, the Trilateral Commission, as a non-governmental organization, can provide information that helps to reinforce coalitions that promote the long-run self-interest. Just as the Cecchini report in Europe helped to dramatize the costs of "non-Europe" and thus provide an impetus for further European

CARL A. RUDISILL LIBRARY
LENOIR-RHYNE COLLEGE

integration, so the Trilateral Commission can study and illustrate the costs of "non-Trilateralism."

We have already mentioned a number of formal institutions which can make major contributions to furthering the long-run self-interests of the Trilateral countries: the United Nations Security Council, the World Bank and IMF, the GATT, the International Atomic Energy Agency, the Bank for European Reconstruction and Development, and many others. Informal studies and consultations among the Trilateral countries can make these organizations more effective. In the context of the UN Security Council, for example, we have already suggested supplementary informal procedures that would allow Japan to play a larger role.

In addition to coordinating their positions within larger organizations, the Trilateral countries need to look more closely at their own cooperation. Both the Organization for Economic Cooperation and Development (OECD) in Paris and the Group of Seven (G-7)—particularly the annual Summit process—can play larger roles. The OECD is useful, for example, in conducting studies of issues that concern the Trilateral countries, in multilateral examination of national policies, and in coordinating procedures for development assistance. The annual Summit not only focuses the attention of top-level leaders on common economic and political problems once a year, but the run-up to the Summit also helps to set the agenda of common concerns and issues for the national bureaucracies. Two changes might make the Group of Seven a more effective institution. One would be to establish a permanent secretariat that would spread the consultations more evenly over the year rather than focusing solely on the Summit. The other is to increase the role of political directors in the consultation process, both for the Summit and more regularly during the year.

Although the Summits were originally focused solely on the global economy, over time the countries found that there were more and more political issues that required their common discussion. It now seems appropriate to institutionalize this development by arranging for regular meetings of the political directors or undersecretaries of the Summit countries. One problem with a greater role for the Group of Seven is that it does not include all twelve members of the European Community. Thus it should be seen as an interim institution until Europe can act as one, and in that interim the four European members of the Summit Seven must insure close consultations with their partners in Europe. The problem is somewhat

CARL A. RUDISILL LIBRARY
LENOIR-RHYNE COLLEGE

alleviated by the fact that the President of the Commission and the head of the Council of Ministers are invited to attend the G-7 meetings, thus providing another avenue for the smaller European countries to make their voices heard. In short, no institution will be perfectly adapted to meeting the new challenges of the 1990s. Rather the Trilateral countries will need a variety of institutions, both formal and informal, to deal with the changing agenda.

10. Greater Decision-Sharing and Burden-Sharing

The problem of burden-sharing among allies is not new to the Trilateral countries. As an earlier Trilateral report—*Sharing International Responsibilities*[2]—pointed out in 1983, economists have long worried about the provision of collective or public goods. A public good is one which, if produced by any member or members of a group, benefits every member in the group. When governments rely on voluntary contributions to support the costs of public goods, many individuals fail to contribute fully, since they know they are likely to receive the benefits whether they contribute fully or not. This is the "free rider" problem. A classic example arises in the area of security. If one nation provides security, others are tempted to accept it as a free gift or to resist paying in full their share. Thus there are always likely to be frictions over burden-sharing in the provision of public goods, whether it be within a country or among a group of countries. During the Cold War, there were constant disputes between the United States and its allies as to whether the allies were doing enough to share the burden of common defense against the Soviet Union. Friction over burden-sharing is one of the factors that could feed inward-turning attitudes in the United States in the post-Cold War period. Since the largest state is always crucial in the provision of public goods, such attitudes could become a problem for other Trilateral countries.

The inherently difficult task of agreeing on burden-sharing becomes even more difficult when the common threat is not so clear. Given the diffusion of perceived threats and the domestic dimensions of many transnational challenges, it will be more difficult in the 1990s to define common interests. Before a burden can be defined, there must be agreement on the common interest. While the Americans retain preponderant military power, it will be tempting for the United

---

[2] Nobuhiko Ushiba, Graham Allison, and Thierry de Montbrial, *Sharing International Responsibilities Among the Trilateral Countries* (1983).

States to assert what is the common interest and then demand that others share the burden of supporting it. But other countries may not perceive the situation in the same way and therefore may legitimately resist taking up the burden. For a public good such as maintaining an open trading system, the burden to be shared involves more than writing checks—it also involves important domestic adjustments.

Before there can be decisions on burden-sharing, there needs to be agreement on defining the collective ends and appropriate means. During the Gulf War, the burden-sharing was impressive,[3] but the process left much to be desired. This brings us back to institutions and consultations. Burden-sharing will require decision-sharing, and formulas for sharing agreed burdens will have to take into account a wide variety of activities. The Japanese concept of "comprehensive security" may be of some help here.[4] Through consultations, it will be necessary to develop an agreement on the wide variety of challenges that the Trilateral countries face and the appropriate responses. Among the dimensions of "comprehensive security" will be defense against the residual Soviet threat, contributions to United Nations

---

[3] As of April 1, 1991, financial and in-kind assistance committed to the United States for Desert Shield and Desert Storm totalled over $53 billion. While about $37 billion of this is from Gulf states, Japanese and German contributions are also large—together totalling over $16 billion. The full incremental cost to the United States of Desert Storm and Desert Shield has not been determined, but allied assistance is likely to cover 80 percent or more of the total. Some Trilateral countries also committed financial and in-kind assistance to other Trilateral countries (aside from the United States) participating heavily in the coalition military effort, such as Germany's commitments to the United Kingdom valued at over $800 million.

There was broad participation in extraordinary economic assistance to countries disrupted economically by the Gulf crisis. The U.S. Treasury put the total committed as of March 11 (primarily to Egypt, Turkey and Jordan) at $15.7 billion. While about $9.7 billion of this total was committed by Gulf states, about $3.2 billion was committed by the European Community and its members and $2.2 billion by Japan.

There has also been broad participation, after Desert Storm, in emergency aid for refugees and internally displaced Iraqi populations. The European Community noted on May 29 that the EC and its member-states had commited $602 million for these purposes. The United States had pledged $213 million and Japan $100 million.

[4] "Comprehensive security" is one of two general concepts or principles (the other is "rough equivalence") around which the authors of the 1983 *Sharing International Responsibilities* report organized their conclusions. Comprehensive security "recognizes the variety of contributions needed for international order and progress, and helps avoid the recriminations which are inevitable if attention is restricted to a single dimension....It provides the opportunity for a division of labor that exploits comparative advantage. Comprehensive security can be a slogan for avoiding certain kind of contributions. But properly understood, this concept should broaden appreciation of the multi-dimensional challenge we face." (p. 74)

collective security and peacekeeping activities, official development assistance (and assistance to specific areas such as Eastern Europe or the Soviet Union), measures to improve the international economy, and a number of others.

What all these dimensions have in common is the need for deeper consultations and greater decision-sharing. This is an area where the United States in particular will need to adapt its attitudes, for while it may be the largest power in the post-Cold War world, no large country will be able to achieve what it wants unilaterally. If the United States wants others to join in coalitions and share the burden of common challenges, it will have to use multilateral institutions to develop the habit of decision-sharing. If others pay, they will have a right to say. Another way of putting it is that while others were free riders, the Americans had full control of the steering wheel. If others pay a fare, they will have a greater say about where the bus will go.

An appendix to this report updates a portion of the appendix in the 1983 *Sharing International Responsibilities* report concerning contributions of the partners.

THE ROLE OF THE TRILATERAL COMMISSION

The changing agenda of international politics suggests a changing role for the Trilateral Commission. The diversity of the challenges means that the educational role of the Commission will be greater than ever. Studies that clarify and illustrate the nature of the new challenges can contribute to shaping opinion in the Trilateral democracies, but reports often get lost in the noise of modern life. Thus the Commission should consider ongoing study groups to address these challenges and seek points of access into each other's societies in order to promote common or cooperative solutions to these issues. In that sense, the Trilateral Commission will need to think of itself as helping to formulate transnational coalitions that advance the common good.

Such a Trilateral coalition will need to define new common objectives. How do cultural and societal differences affect our ability to promote common values? What are the common problems or challenges and how should the burden of meeting them be shared? What are the common standards by which we judge the appropriateness of the actions of different countries? To what extent do they fit with some larger concept of comprehensive security? In addition, the Trilateral Commission can help to provide channels of information about how our different democracies respond to common problems.

To provide ongoing channels of communication as well as encourage transnational coalitions to promote common interests, the Commission might consider the development of three study groups which would meet between the annual plenaries and report to the plenary. One group on common security would deal with the challenges related to the residual threats posed by the existence of Soviet (or Russian) military power, as well as the problems arising from regional disputes and the difficulties encountered in UN collective security and peacekeeping operations. A second study group might deal with the continuing problems of economic interdependence, finding ways to enhance the prospects for open trade and investment as well as to create a degree of stability in international monetary and financial systems. The third group could deal with global issues related to increasing transnational interdependence.[5] These issues defy the traditional categories of military security or economic prosperity, and include global ecology, transnational social problems, and world population and resource balances. To insure a broad perspective, such groups (as well as the annual meeting) should include qualified experts from other relevant regions.

In short, the 1990s environment for cooperation among the Trilateral countries will be less hospitable than the 1970s and 1980s. In the absence of an overarching, easily dramatized external threat, the natural tendencies of citizens in democracies will be to turn toward their domestic affairs, and they will be more likely to see problems through parochial perspectives. But the Trilateral Commission can help to dramatize the costs of non-Trilateralism, e.g., the cost of allowing the world economy to break into separate blocs, and can help to organize informed responses. The conditions for Trilateral cooperation will become more difficult but the need for it will become even greater.

---

[5] As this report is completed in June 1991, three such groups have been created and are developing their work programs.

APPENDIX:
CONTRIBUTIONS OF THE PARTNERS

The 1983 report to the Trilateral Commission entitled *Sharing International Responsibilities*—prepared by Nobuhiko Ushiba, Graham Allison, and Thierry de Montbrial—included an extensive appendix of quantitative indicators relevant to analysis under three headings: benefits of partnership, capacities of the partners, and contributions of the partners. We agree with the 1983 authors that "efforts to develop agreed upon definitions and yardsticks are often lost in terminological—and political—thickets of extraordinary complexity....What constitutes contributions of a country towards the achievement of common objectives? And how should they be judged? In absolute terms? In relation to capacities? Relative to other countries?" Nevertheless, it is important to develop such indicators to the extent possible. Even if no single agreed conception emerges, some misconceptions and oversimplifications in the debate about these matters can be set aside.

The following appendix is not a comprehensive updating of that earlier effort, but it does attempt to update and extend the set of indicators relating to contributions of the partners. The first two tables present military manpower and defense expenditures. The following five tables relate to assistance to developing countries. The final table relates to the relative energy intensity of national economies. The argument was made during our work that reductions in energy intensity and lower absolute levels are positive international contributions in that they represent less profligate use of energy resources and less dependence (assuming for the moment that everything else is equal) on external sources of supply.

Table 1: **Military Manpower**[a]

	Armed Forces (thousands)		as % of Population		as % of NATO Total		as % of Total	
	1981–82[b]	1990–91	1981–82[b]	1990–91	1981–82[b]	1990–91	1981–82[b]	1990–91
United States	2049	2118	0.9	0.9	41.5	40.4	39.6	38.5
Canada	79	90	0.3	0.3	1.6	1.7	1.5	1.6
France	505	461	0.9	0.8	10.2	8.8	9.7	8.4
Germany	495	469	0.8	0.8	10.0	8.9	9.6	8.5
United Kingdom	344	306	0.6	0.5	7.0	5.8	6.6	5.6
Italy	366	390	0.6	0.7	7.4	7.4	7.1	7.1
Japan	243	249	0.2	0.2	—	—	4.7	4.5
NATO Europe	2805	3039	0.9	0.8	56.9	57.9	54.2	55.3
NATO	4963	5247	0.9	0.8	100.0	100.0	95.3	95.5
NATO Plus Japan	5177	5496	0.7	0.7	—	—	100.0	100.0

[a] Active forces.
[b] Excludes Spain, which had not yet joined the North Atlantic Alliance.

Source: International Institute for Strategic Studies, *The Military Balance 1981–82* (London: IISS, 1981) and *The Military Balance 1990–91* (London: IISS, 1990).

Table 2: **Defense Expenditures**[a]

	Total[b] (US$ billions)		Per Capita[b] (US$)		as % of GDP		as % of NATO Total		as % of Total	
	1980[c]	1989	1980[c]	1989	1980[c]	1988	1980[c]	1989	1980[c]	1989
United States	206.6	289.1	917	1162	5.4	6.1	59.6	63.3	56.3	59.5
Canada	7.2	9.9	297	373	1.8	2.0	2.1	2.2	2.0	2.0
France	32.2	36.4	599	645	4.0	3.8	9.3	8.0	8.8	7.5
Germany[d]	33.8	35.0	548	579	3.3	2.9	9.7	7.7	9.2	7.2
United Kingdom	31.1	34.5	556	608	4.7	4.3	9.0	7.5	8.5	7.1
Italy	14.2	20.8	248	363	2.1	2.5	4.1	4.6	3.9	4.3
Japan	20.1	29.4	171	237	0.9	1.0	—	—	5.5	6.0
NATO Europe	133.0	157.7	405	414	—	—	38.4	34.5	36.7	32.4
NATO	346.8	456.8	600	695	—	—	100.0	100.0	94.5	94.0
NATO Plus Japan	366.9	486.2	528	623	—	—	—	—	100.0	100.0

[a] Significant differences exist among national definitions of defense expenditures. This is particularly true between the NATO countries and Japan. The standard NATO accounting formula (followed by most NATO members) includes items such as veterans' benefits and pensions. The Japanese formula does not. International comparisons—such as the data compiled annually by the International Institute for Strategic Studies used here—usually follow the guidelines employed by national sources. Thus, Japan's defense figures tend to be understated relative to NATO country figures. According to most experts, Japan's 1980 defense budget, measured by NATO's standards, would amount to 1.5–1.7% of Japanese GNP.

[b] In US$ millions, at 1988 prices and exchange-rates.

[c] Excludes Spain, which had not yet joined the North Atlantic Alliance.

[d] West German figures. Figures do not include aid to West Berlin.

Sources: International Institute for Strategic Studies, *The Military Balance 1981–82* (London: IISS, 1981), International Institute for Strategic Studies, *The Military Balance 1990–91* (London: IISS, 1990) and *SIPRI Yearbook 1990: World Armaments and Disarmament* (Oxford University Press,

Table 3: Official Development Assistance (ODA)
(US$ millions)

	Total ODA		Bilateral		Multilateral		Total ODA as % of GNP		Total ODA as % of DAC Total		Total ODA Per Capita (US$)	
	1978–80ᵃ	1989	1978–80	1989	1978–80	1989	1978–80	1989	1978–80	1989	1978–80	1989
Canada	1064	2320	633	1581	431	739	0.47	0.44	4.6	5.0	44.5	88.4
France	3439	7450	2896	6135	542	1315	0.60	0.78	14.7	16.0	64.3	132.7
Germany	3102	4949	2029	3175	1073	1773	0.42	0.41	13.3	10.6	50.9	79.8
Italy	444	3613	43	2189	401	1424	0.13	0.42	1.9	7.7	7.8	62.8
Japan	2751	8949	1837	6763	915	2186	0.27	0.32	11.8	19.2	23.6	72.7
United Kingdom	1825	2587	1132	1463	693	1124	0.43	0.31	7.8	5.5	32.6	45.2
United States	5829	7659	3972	6810	1856	849	0.24	0.15	24.9	16.4	25.6	30.8
Total DAC	23388	46679	15863	34197	7525	12483	0.36	0.33	100.0	100.0	34.5	65.1
ECᵇ	1132	2879	970	2647	162	231	—	—	4.8	6.2	—	—

ᵃ annual average.
ᵇ EC as an institution, rather than as the sum of its constituent states.

Sources: Development Co-operation 1990 Report (OECD, 1990); World Development Report 1982 (The World Bank, 1982).

Table 4: **Total Resource Flows (TRF) to Developing Countries**
(US$ millions)

	Total Public Official Flows[b]		Grants by Private Voluntary Agencies		Private Flows at Market Terms		TRF[a]		TRF as % of GNP		TRF as % of DAC Total		TRF Per Capita (US$)	
	1978–80	1989	1978–80	1989	1978–80	1989	1978–80	1989	1978–80	1989	1978–80	1989	1978–80	1989
Canada	1565	2687	95	238	1035	-208	2695	2718	1.20	0.51	3.6	3.2	112.8	103.6
France	3903	7450	26	106[c]	5512	-783[c]	9441	7215[c]	1.65	0.76[c]	12.8	8.4	176.5	128.5
Germany	3423	5978	365	679	4720	5495	8509	12152	1.15	1.01	11.5	14.2	139.7	196.0
Italy	848	4736	1	42	2920	974	3769	5752	1.08	0.67	5.1	6.7	66.2	100.0
Japan	4031	10472	21	122	4321	13502	8374	24096	0.84	0.85	11.3	28.2	71.7	195.7
United Kingdom	1936	3046	95	262	9653	387	11684	3695	2.75	0.45	15.8	4.3	209.0	64.6
United States	6991	7659	1087	2255[c]	8199	3203[c]	16276	17505[c]	0.67	0.36[c]	22.0	20.5	71.5	70.4
Total DAC	27906	53057	2019	4234	44094	28261	74019	85552	1.13	0.64	100.0	100.0	109.3	119.4
EC[d]	1298	3052	—	—	—	—	—	—	—	—	—	—	—	—

[a] TRF are defined as Total Public Official Flows plus Grants by Private Voluntary Agencies plus Private Flows at Market Terms. Total Public Official Flows include both bilateral and multilateral ODA, as well as Other Official Flows, including official export credits, equities and other assets.

[b] Annual average.

[c] 1988 figure.

[d] EC as an institution, rather than as the sum of its constituent states.

Sources: Development Co-operation 1990 Report (OECD, 1990); *World Development Report 1982* (The World Bank, 1982).

TABLE 5: **Technical Cooperation**

Expenditures

	Total (US$ millions)		% of Total DAC		Per Capita (US$)	
	1980	1989	1980	1989	1980	1989
Canada	99	246	1.8	2.3	4.1	9.4
France	1825	2604	33.4	24.7	34.1	46.4
Germany	991	1451	18.1	13.7	16.3	23.4
Italy	55	352	1.0	3.3	1.0	6.1
Japan	278	1348	5.1	12.8	2.4	10.9
United Kingdom	507	608	9.3	5.8	9.1	10.6
United States	724	2141	13.2	20.3	3.2	8.6
Total DAC	5472	10557	100.0	100.0	8.1	14.7

Publicly Financed Personnel[a]

	Total		% of Total DAC		Per Capita[b]	
	1980	1987	1980	1987	1980	1987
Canada	2057	4647[c]	3.0	5.9	86.1	181.2
France	17291	12970[c]	25.2	16.4	323.2	233.1
Germany	5850	7117	8.5	9.0	96.1	116.5
Italy	1597	3374	2.3	4.3	28.1	58.9
Japan	8215	15370	12.0	19.5	70.3	125.9
United Kingdom	7614	3162	11.1	4.0	136.2	55.5
United States	11477	21093[c]	16.7	26.7	50.4	86.5
Total DAC	68700[d]	79000[cd]	100.0	100.0	101.5	111.7

[a] Not including students and trainees.
[b] Number per 1 million population.
[c] 1986 figure.
[d] OECD Secretariat estimate in whole or in part.

Sources: Development Co-operation 1990 Report (OECD, 1990); *World Development Report 1982* (The World Bank, 1982).

Note: DAC states are those on the OECD's Development Assistance Committee: Australia, Austria, Belgium, Canada, Denmark, Finland, France, Germany, Ireland, Italy, Japan, Netherlands, New Zealand, Norway, Sweden, Switzerland, United Kingdom, United States.

Table 6: **Multilateral ODA**

(US$ millions, 1989)

	UN	World Bank	Total[a]	as % of DAC Total	Per Capita (US$)
Canada	274	182	739	5.9	28.2
France	113	352	1315	10.5	23.4
Germany	217	620	1773	14.2	28.6
Italy	241	540	1424	11.4	24.8
Japan	501	931	2186	17.5	17.8
United Kingdom	190	292	1124	9.0	19.7
United States	610	—	850	6.8	3.4
Total DAC	3410	3727	12483	100.0	17.4

[a] Including other multilateral agencies as well.

Source: Development Co-operation 1990 Report (OECD, 1990).

Table 7: **Other ODA Indicators**

(1988–89 average)

	% of Total DAC ODA	% of Total DAC GNP	Grant Equivalent of Total ODA as % of GNP	Aid Appropriations as % of Central Government Budget	Multilateral ODA[a] as % of GNP
Canada	4.9	3.6	0.48	1.93	0.15
France	15.1	7.0	0.69	2.94	0.07
Germany	10.1	8.8	0.39[b]	2.45	0.07
Italy	7.2	6.1	0.41	0.92	0.09
Japan	19.1	20.8	0.28	1.24	0.09
United Kingdom	5.5	6.0	0.33	1.16	0.08
United States	18.8	36.8	0.18	0.65	0.04
Total DAC	100.0	100.0	0.34[b]	1.25[b]	0.08

[a] Not including EC.
[b] OECD Secretariat estimate in whole or in part.

Source: Development Co-operation 1990 Report (OECD, 1990).

TABLE 8: **Energy Intensity[a] of G-7 National Economies**

	1980	1983	1986	1989	% change 1980-89
Canada	28.1	25.6	24.5	24.1	-14%
United States	21.9	19.6	18.1	17.9	-18%
France	12.3	10.8	10.9	10.1	-18%
W. Germany	14.6	13.8	14.1	12.6	-14%
Italy	11.0	10.1	9.9	9.7	-12%
United Kingdom	16.6	14.4	14.1	13.5	-19%
Japan	11.5	9.7	9.4	9.0	-22%

[a] Primary energy consumption in thousands of BTUs per dollar of real GDP.

Sources: Energy consumption information has been taken from the 1989 *International Energy Annual* of the Energy Information Administration in the U.S. Department of Energy. The 1989 consumption figures are preliminary. GDP (in constant 1985 national currency units) has been taken from the IMF's *International Financial Statistics,* in particular from the 1990 *Yearbook* and June 1991 edition. (The one exception is the 1989 GDP of Japan, an estimate taken from the 1991 edition of the World Bank's *World Tables.*) To convert national currency units into U.S. dollars, we have taken the average of the 1980, 1983, 1986 and 1989 exchange rates presented in the *IFS Yearbook* for each of the relevant currencies.